Sacraments and Liturgy

Faith and the Future
General Editor: David Nicholls

Choices
Ethics and the Christian
David Brown

Church and Nation
Peter Cornwell

Pastoral Care and the Parish
Peter Davie

The Faith Abroad
John D. Davies

Church, Ministry and Unity
A Divine Commission
James E. Griffiss

The Authority of Divine Love
Richard Harries

The Bible
Fountain and Well of Truth
John Muddiman

Faith, Prayer and Devotion
Ralph Townsend

Sacraments and Liturgy
The Outward Signs
Louis Weil

Sacraments and Liturgy
The Outward Signs

A Study in Liturgical Mentality

Louis Weil

Basil Blackwell

First published 1983
Basil Blackwell Publisher Limited
108 Cowley Road, Oxford OX4 1JF, England

British Library Cataloguing in Publication Data
Weil, Louis
    Sacraments and liturgy.—(Faith and the future)
    1. Sacraments—Church of England
    I. Title   II. Series
    265   BX5148

    ISBN 0-631-13192-2
    ISBN 0-631-13229-5 Pbk

Typesetting by Cambrian Typesetters, Aldershot, Hants
Printed in Great Britain by T.J. Press Ltd, Padstow

Contents

Foreword

This book is one of a series whose writers consider some important aspects of Christianity in the contemporary scene and in so doing draw inspiration from the Catholic revival in the Anglican Communion which began in Oxford one hundred and fifty years ago. This revival — with its thinkers, pastors, prophets, social reformers and not a few who have been held to be saints — has experienced changes in the understanding of the Christian faith since the time of the Tractarians and has none the less borne witness to themes which are deep and unchanging. Among these are the call to holiness, the communion of saints, the priesthood of the Church and its ministers and a sacramental religion, both otherworldly and with revolutionary claims upon man's social life.

I am myself convinced that the renewal of the Church for today and tomorrow needs a deep recovery of these themes of Catholic tradition and a vision of their contemporary application. The books of this series are designed for the help they give. Many are thirsty but 'the well is deep'.

+ Michael Ramsey

Introduction

The essential characteristic of worship is wonderfully simple: worship is the way in which human beings express the ultimate place of God in their lives. Although many generations ago the word was used generally in regard to acts of respect toward honoured persons, it gradually came to be used only in reference to religious acts, referring to the whole complex of words and rites by which a believing people praise and honour the God who is the foundation of their faith.

It is obvious from only a casual survey of human history that men and women have expressed this praise and honour of God in a highly diverse pattern which reflects not only the influence of the diversity of cultures, but also the impact of varied social and temperamental factors. When we consider the phenomenon of worship within the Christian tradition, we are immediately engaged by its central article of faith, the Incarnation, the assertion that God has acted within human history through a radical identification with Jesus of Nazareth. This assertion establishes what we might call 'the principle of the Incarnation'. By this principle, Christianity is seen as a unity. All the various aspects of Christian theology are signs of this principle and find their coherence in the claim that God uses the material, created world as the means of his self-revelation. According to this principle, human beings become the primary agents of God's action in the world, and, in a complementary way, all material things bear the potential of being instruments and signs of the grace of God present and active in human life.

The implications of this principle for Christian worship

are far-reaching. The worship of God cannot be only or even primarily a mental activity, but must involve the whole range of characteristics which make a person human: mind, of course, but also the feelings, and the body with all its senses. The principle of the Incarnation implies that an act of worship, the offering of praise and honour to God because of his ultimacy in regard to all that exists, should signify the engagement of the whole person and the whole created world in a divine/human encounter. It is not only through ideas and words that human beings express their most basic attitudes. Love involves the body, the whole being, if it is truly a giving of self to the other, and so does the act of worship. In this perspective, the physical elements which we use take on a dramatic significance, not as an end in themselves, but as integral to the total act.

To speak in this way of Christian worship is to point to its fundamental sacramentality. The sacramental nature of certain specific liturgical actions is a sign of the underlying sacramentality of the Church itself. The Church is the faith-society made up of all those who have been incorporated into God's action in Christ. The sacraments are the faith-actions of those same people of God who have become the human instruments of God's purposes. To speak of the sacraments in this way in general is to see them not as isolated religious acts but as signs of a common faith and life in Christ.

The most common definition of a sacrament speaks of 'an outward and visible sign of an inward and spiritual grace'. This definition must be understood, however, within the wider framework of the Church's life spoken of above, or else there can result a separation of sacramental theory from sacramental practice, and of individual piety from the corporate experience. The celebration of a sacrament takes place within the context of an assembly of faithful people. The full meaning of the sacraments involves an awareness of the complex social and cultural realities in which the members of the Church are always involved. Sacraments are not purely intellectual activities. They are celebrated by specific human persons in a specific social context and all this multiplicity of factors shapes their participation in the meaning of the sign.

From this perspective, it is impossible to discuss sacramental theory apart from liturgical practice. Our understanding of the meaning of the Eucharist, for example, is inevitably formed by our experience of the way in which the Eucharist is celebrated, and that is in turn influenced by a range of cultural and historical factors. The ways in which the Eucharist is celebrated not only vary in regard to details of ritual, but also reflect significant differences of attitude in regard to Church and ministry. The Church's life unfolds within a context in which factors which are not explicitly theological have dramatic impact upon the meaning ascribed to its acts of worship. If liturgical practice is affected by such factors in significant ways and over a period of time, the Christian community's understanding of the fundamental meaning is modified and, as history demonstrates, often distorted.

If the liturgical renewal of this century is to be of any real and abiding significance, its most urgent task is not a preoccupation with liturgical details, but rather the development of a perceptive awareness of the integral relation between sacramental meaning and liturgical practice. The implications of the rediscovered meaning for the reform of our pastoral liturgical norms is far-reaching. The old adage, 'the law of prayer constitutes the law of faith', impels us toward a serious liturgical stewardship in this regard.

The purpose of this book is modest. The revision of official liturgical books in all the major Christian churches has, within the past several years, provoked a significant reaction. The new rites are expressions of the principles of sacramental theology which have emerged in a general ecumenical context in this century. But the reactions to the introduction of those rites at the level of parochial worship have demonstrated how much the liturgy had become the occasion, for many Christians, for the exercise of private piety. A sacramental theology which affirms the primary importance of corporate worship has run directly

3

into an entrenched, and often unconscious, individualistic piety. As with so many undertakings, this project has turned out to be more complex than the author anticipated, but it is hoped that an exploration of the factors which shaped the piety of the Oxford Tractarians will shed light upon the contemporary situation, especially for those of us who are their heirs. In many ways the affirmations of the Tractarians about the Church, sacraments and worship raised some of the primary questions upon which liturgical renewal today is based.

1 Retrospect

Human history is shaped by numerous forces. Whether it be the life of an individual, a family, or a whole society, there is a marvellous chemistry involved in the shaping of attitudes and lines of action. Consequently, it is a complex task to sort out which factors have been most crucial in defining the character of a movement or event, especially since these involve the mutual influences effected by the interworking of many lives.

In the face of this complexity, it would be tempting to oversimplify or to take too narrow a perspective. But movements and events must not be separated from the wider historical perspective. They are always part of a tapestry of interwoven factors. They are shaped, often in subtle yet critical ways, by the wider framework out of which they come to birth. Cultural, social and political dynamics inevitably contribute to the shape of the movement even when they seem to pertain to quite distinct areas of human activity. This assertion is as true of the Oxford Movement as of any other. An adequate assessment of its impact requires some sense of this larger perspective.

The understanding of liturgy and the sacraments which was taught by the leaders of the Oxford Movement, even where there were differences in point of view, would seem to be a simple matter to set forth. By and large, we have been conditioned to think of these issues in terms of a rather narrow range of cultic activity within the life of the Church. A catechism-style approach to doctrinal questions, even when set out at an advanced intellectual level, has shaped an expectation that such matters may be conveniently expressed through a set of definitions. Useful as such definitions may be as a point of departure, they are dangerous when, as has so often been the case, they have been viewed as adequate statements about the realities to which they point. What the early Fathers spoke of as the mysteries of Christian faith are reduced to static cultic rites caught within narrow religious categories, and we are left with no mystery at all.

The purpose of this study is to indicate how far-reaching and all-encompassing are the implications of liturgical/sacramental actions within the whole range of the Church's life, and even beyond the general presuppositions of the Church rooted in the cultural fabric of a particular period. In this perspective, the concerns of the Oxford leaders are part of an ongoing process within the Church's life in every age to realize the implications of the Gospel in a given historical situation. The liturgical concerns of the Oxford Movement are far more important than merely issues of ritual detail. They are ordered toward the renewal of the Church's self-understanding. Our purpose here is to consider the primary factors which shaped those concerns, and then to look at these matters from the perspective of contemporary liturgical and sacramental renewal.

In order to evaluate these concerns, we must try to see how the Oxford leaders were men of their time, shaped by the broadly cultural forces which affected everyone in society, often in unconscious ways. It is precisely in the presuppositions of a society, or even of the leaders of a movement, that we see the complexity of the factors which shaped their attitudes. It is not merely a question of the temperaments and convictions of a few men, but rather the shaping of those diverse temperaments in relation to the larger social landscape. Many revolutionary developments took place in nineteenth-century society which had direct impact upon the shaping of a certain type of religious temperament which longed for the stability and integrity which were believed to characterize an earlier and holier age. But to see the rooting of the Oxford Movement in the nostalgia of Romanticism in no way implies the rejection of some important insights which the Tractarians developed concerning the nature of the Church and its worship, insights which were in several points anticipatory of the central concerns of liturgical and sacramental renewal in the last decades of the twentieth century.

BACKGROUND TO THE MOVEMENT

The immediate causes of the origin of the Oxford Movement are found in the malaise which gripped the Church of England during the first decades of the nineteenth century. A fuller perspective to the movement is gained from a consideration of the major cultural forces which were at work during the period, and which were themselves conditioned by earlier developments. Although it is true that the genesis of the movement was in response to the desperately impaired state of the Church, the character of the response was shaped by the general cultural situation.

The Enlightenment left a decisive mark upon the English Church. During the last decades of the seventeenth century, there was a growing discontent within the Church. Advances in science raised doubts about some of the traditional dogmas of Christianity. It was a period which extolled the role of reason as the means of ascertaining the truth. Earlier in the century, men such as Lancelot Andrewes (1555–1626) had insisted upon the primacy of faith over reason in matters of Christian doctrine, but gradually this gave way to an increasing emphasis upon the place of reason in human life. Reason was held to be the voice of God and the final arbiter in the determination of truth.

At first there was no direct conflict between the growth of rationalism and Christian faith. Christianity was held to complement the findings of reason, but the implications of faith were seen more and more in the realm of the moral life rather than in the holding of specific Christian doctrines. In the Church of England, this view had been anticipated in the seventeenth century by the Latitudinarians, who placed ultimate importance upon reason in all matters,

7

including matters of religion. They shied away from any intensity of expression in religious attitudes, including the phenomenon coming to be known as 'enthusiasm'. Their view of religion was as part of the ordered world of the Enlightenment, the essentials being few in number, and issuing forth in a moral life.

The emphasis upon reason in matters of religion, however, laid the ground for a yet more fundamental attack upon Christian faith in the rise of deism. Reason was taken as the basis for rejecting any element of the supernatural or mysterious in Christianity. Any special beliefs which could not be verified from nature, such as the belief in miracles, had to be put aside as a reflection of the religion of mankind's immaturity. Since all truth could be found in the natural religion of human reason, there was no need for belief in divine revelation of any kind. It was abhorrent to the deists that God should be claimed to manipulate the created world and not to respect its internal natural law which was itself his creation. Within the Church of England, a response to the deists was given by William Law (1686–1761) and Joseph Butler (1692–1752), who wrote as advocates of the role of revelation in Christian faith. They acknowledged the importance played by reason as a human faculty, but insisted upon its limitations in religion.

The rationalism which dominated the spirit of the time had its effect. During the eighteenth century, the Church was weakened by an overriding indifferentism in religious matters and was generally viewed as a department of the state, with a consequent loss of a sense of its spiritual and supernatural vocation. Allowing for a few exceptions, the members of the episcopate were often more concerned with political than religious priorities. The bishops spent much of their time in London involved with the affairs of government, and were able to give only superficial attention to the sacramental and administrative needs of their dioceses. Many of the local clergy were poorly educated and badly supported economically. Pluralism compounded the problems by permitting men with powerful connections to hold a number of livings at the same time. This abuse

8

gave them substantial income but meant, of course, that they were usually absent from these pastoral responsibilities, the parochial work being left to underpaid and demoralized curates.

The public worship of the Church in such circumstances lacked the vitality which springs from a strong inner life. It was for the most part formal, with rites subject to abbreviation by the minister at will. Though often of great length, the sermons of the time are criticized in the literature of the period for their poor quality, often degenerating to mere moralistic harangues. Sacramental practice had little importance in an ecclesiastical structure with no sense of the sacramental nature of its own life. Rationalism had left little place for religious feeling in the life of the believer or much support for religious practices which made claims upon more than the rational element in man. By and large it was a time of complacency among the leaders of the Church. They were more concerned with personal privilege and prestige than with the spiritual needs of the people.

THE EVANGELICAL MOVEMENT

The life and ministry of John Wesley (1703–91) was a providential response to the state of the Church. For our purposes, it suffices to note that the Wesleyan movement was a powerful and effective answer to the dry rationalism which dominated the Church at that time. Through Wesley the valid role of religious feeling in the life of faith was reaffirmed. But the impact of his controversial preaching was such that it attracted hostility from the clergy, and pulpits were closed to him. The phenomenal growth of the movement led, despite Wesley's wishes, to its separation from the Church of England. Although many evangelicals remained in the established Church, the alienation of the Methodists was a tragic loss.

The Wesleyan movement burst upon England at the high noon of rationalism, and the established Church was unable with its rigid structures to deal with this intense sign of new spiritual vitality. Rationalism had left the leadership of the Church ill equipped to deal with the 'enthusiasm' engendered by such evangelical preaching. In this respect, the movement inaugurated by Wesley offers an interesting parallel to the origins of the Oxford Movement, not in regard to doctrinal concerns, but as religious protests. Both linked religious faith to the heart. Both movements gave serious consideration to religious feeling and sentiment as the source of a life of devotion and holiness. What the Oxford Movement added, and what so clearly distinguished it, was a sacramental view of the Church. Yet also here we see a path which had been re-opened by Wesley with his strong emphasis upon frequent reception of Communion. Although often conditioned by a highly individual piety, this emphasis clearly recovered for English Evangelicals an awareness of the importance of the sacramental life for Christian faith. Exploration of the further implications of that recovery with regard to the nature of the Church was a step to be taken by the Oxford divines in the next century.

THE INDUSTRIAL REVOLUTION

Although the Evangelical movement had significant impact upon religiously disposed people in England, there were other factors at work in the culture of more far-reaching influence upon society as a whole. During the last decades of the eighteenth century the advent of what is known as the Industrial Revolution brought about social changes of the greatest magnitude. In effect, the whole inherited social order came to be radically changed.

The Industrial Revolution was in many ways a kind of culmination of the Enlightenment and a major turning point in history. It eventually encompassed technological, economic and social factors which touched every level of society. The advances of science which were the fruit of the Enlightenment showed mankind to be capable of submitting the physical world to its own intentions. The ordering of this new knowledge in the practical realm transformed society from an agrarian to an industrial life-style. The new inventions brought large numbers of people into the expanding industrial areas. The tradition of individual craftsmanship which had characterized the labour of previous generations was replaced by a dehumanizing monotony in which the worker was seen as little more than a machine, leaving nothing of a personal imprint upon the product.

The social changes inaugurated in England by the Industrial Revolution find a parallel in the impact of the French Revolution, not only in France but in Europe as a whole. Whereas the advance in industrial development came earlier and developed more quickly in England than on the Continent, the revolution in France also had a transforming effect on more than merely political structures, and was also, from an intellectual point of view, an offspring of the Enlightenment with its emphasis on the worth of the individual and a consequent rejection of human injustice and inequalities.

In both France and England the Church showed itself virtually incapable of creative response to the new situations. In France the Church had been allied to the powers of oppression and consequently saw its power broken in the early stages of the revolution. In England, as we have seen, the Church was similarly allied to the state and pursued its life with complacent indifference. Industrialism brought about major shifts in the population as large numbers of families moved into the areas of newly opened coal mines. Rural dioceses of small population found themselves transformed rapidly by an influx which doubled or tripled the people of an area. The Church was a victim of inertia. It was unable to keep pace with these sudden social changes because of outmoded organizational structures. The number of clergy and buildings was not adequate to expanded populations; but more serious was the fact that the dry rationalism which characterized the established Church made no effective appeal to the new labouring class. The Evangelicals were far more successful in reaching a wide element of British society with their appeal to religious feeling rather than intellect, but a

11

significant segment of society was simply lost at that time because of the Church's inability to set the imperative of ministry above other concerns. The Church had lost any real sense of its identity.

Such a bleak picture must lead inevitably either to collapse or to renewal. As we have seen earlier, currents within the Church are closely related to the movements within society as a whole. It is already obvious that the social as well as the religious situation reflected a wide diversity of attitudes and forces. The general picture in England at the beginning of the nineteenth century is quite complex, but one major force, which itself defies a simple definition, dominated the sensibilities of society for several decades and offers us a perspective to the more immediate factors which shaped the character of the response we know as the Oxford Movement. That force was Romanticism.

2 Romanticism and the Gothic Revival

The last decade of the eighteenth century, under the impact of the French Revolution, saw the questioning of the established orthodoxies of the Enlightenment in regard to the all-sufficiency of human reason for the discovery of truth. Writers began to assert the importance of the imagination and of intuition, and the legitimate role of the emotions in human life. A dramatic sign of this occurred in the arts, as the idea of art as a reflection of the surface order of reality gave way to a perception that art permits access to the inner life and is expressive of that deeper reality with its almost limitless diversity.

Consequently there is no single or unifying style in the art of the Romantic era. There is no one tendency, but rather one finds the signs of many different and often conflicting principles and aspirations. It was a highly creative period which gave importance to individuality of expression as an affirmation of the unique quality of each person. In this sense, it marked a freeing from the rigidities which typified the aesthetic theories of Neo-classicism as the dominant style of the later Enlightenment.

Because of its emphasis upon the importance of the imagination and non-rational faculties, Romanticism has been interpreted as a reaction not only to the Enlightenment but more specifically to the dehumanizing forces represented by the Industrial Revolution. A familiar aspect of Romanticism is its nostalgia for the life-style of pre-industrial society. Its first expressions were literary, often dwelling on the picturesque qualities of ruins, but soon including writings concerned with the age of chivalry, and the publication of poetry of the Middle Ages. These writings attracted a large audience during the later decades of the eighteenth century. By the time the Waverly novels of Walter Scott appeared, there had already been nurtured in England a full-scale appetite for antiquity not only in literature but in archaeology as well.

The Gothic revival is only one dimension of the Romantic movement, associated primarily with its earlier decades and reflecting a nostalgia for a more heroic and a more human age. The revival was a multi-faceted phenomenon reflected not only in popular literature but also in the work of scholars, antiquarians and historians. The most visible expression of the Gothic spirit is found in the impact of the revival upon architecture. There were, of course, great Gothic buildings to be seen in all parts of the country, but they had been left in a state of neglect for about two centuries. In many cases, the new appreciation of the Gothic style led to a desire for restoration, often where knowledge of the subject was far from adequate. But it is useful to note that the Gothic revival in architecture was at least in part indebted to the survival of Gothic buildings from the Middle Ages. Even if these buildings were in poor condition, the style had never been eliminated from the general cultural picture.

We see here an interesting parallel to one of the underlying dynamics of the Oxford Movement in that it reflected a true continuity with the doctrinal views of the old high church party, but now recovered and reaffirmed in the context of the spirit of the Romantic movement. This offers us critical insight into a formative aspect of the theological views of the Oxford leaders. Keble, Newman and Pusey had no intention of proposing a new teaching; it was the reassertion of what they believed to be fundamental to the spirit of Anglicanism, but which had been eclipsed during the previous century both by rationalism and by the subordination of the Church to the authority of the government. The Oxford Movement was pre-eminently a recovery of the authentic tradition, just as the Gothic revival was a recovery of the architecture of the most genuinely Christian of all ages. Romantic sensibilities, however, shaped both these recoveries more deeply than could be grasped at the time.

The earliest stage of Gothic restoration and new construction was rather superficial. The majority of early buildings of the revival were not churches but rather mansions and private houses. In the first place, Gothic appealed to the upper classes, those most likely to have been influenced by the revolution in taste effected by the Romantic movement. Since there were no authentic models for medieval mansions, architects were basically free to construct a building of the required proportions and to decorate it with elements which were associated with the Gothic style and which suggested a degree of antiquity to the family estate and thus to its name.

Very few churches were built between 1760 and 1820. Numerous parochial structures remained from the Middle Ages in the rural areas, adequate to the needs of a religiously indifferent populace. Although the urban population grew during this period, new construction in the cities was rare. Church attendance was low, and the people of the labouring classes were more likely to participate in the worship of the dissenting sects. As we have seen, the Church of England had failed seriously to respond to the pastoral needs of the expanded population of industrial areas. In 1818 the Church Building Society was founded. Within fifteen years over £6 million was spent on new church construction following the Church Building Act of the same year. Of the 214 churches which were erected, four-fifths were in a style characterized as Gothic. The description often meant little more than the incorporation of pointed arches in the construction, for this early series of churches does not so much reflect an enthusiasm for medieval architecture as a concern for economy. These were generally brick buildings designed to accommodate the largest number of people at the least expense. The results were, of course, disappointing. The buildings were criticized as 'mere carpenter's Gothic', and the demand for a more authentic expression was soon to carry the revival along a new path.

A Gothic church was an architectural form which developed in accordance with the liturgical expectations of the Middle Ages. The building itself gave witness to a concept of worship, a sacramental spirituality, which the majority of Anglicans had either rejected or at least ceased to experience under the impact of the rationalistic views of the Enlightenment. The building implied a theology of Church, sacraments and ministry which many Anglicans, including persons in positions of high authority, would have been eager to reject. The Neo-classical church buildings of the seventeenth century were auditory chambers, places in which the sermon was obviously understood to be the primary purpose of the assembly, and in which a sacramental piety found little expression. A Gothic church, especially one faithful to the interior details of disposition, implied a Roman Catholic understanding of worship.

THE WORK OF PUGIN

The person who raised the question of the relation of theology to Gothic architecture was Augustus Welby Pugin (1812–52). Pugin's decision to become a Roman Catholic in 1834 was closely linked to his aesthetic theories. Pugin's analysis of the churches erected by the Commissioners under the Church Building Act was that the mechanical aspect of Gothic architecture was understood but that the underlying principles which influenced the authentic Gothic buildings were lacking. What Pugin was asserting was that Gothic is not simply one style among others available for the choice of an architect, but rather that Gothic is the pre-eminent architectural expression of Catholic faith and piety. Pugin saw an organic connection between architecture and society. This is in fact an underlying sacramental principle which can be applied appropriately to all the material aspects of liturgical worship. Catholic sacramental liturgy is expressive of Catholic faith. Although nurtured by a Romantic nostalgia for things medieval, Pugin moved far beyond that level in his theoretical reflections. The Middle Ages were for him the only truly Christian age, and hence its faith, liturgy, piety, architecture and vesture were the standard, the model according to which all lesser expressions were to be judged. A church is designed for the worship of God and thus fleshes out in its architecture the understanding of worship of the society that built it. For Pugin, a good society will produce beautiful buildings because it holds the true faith.

THE ECCLESIOLOGISTS

In the popular mind the Oxford Movement is often associated with elaborate ceremonial in the liturgy. The introduction of ritual practices generally connected with Roman Catholicism is the commonly held consequence of the Oxford Movement upon Anglican worship, and this is certainly an eminently visible and thus easily recognizable factor.

The fact is, however, that neither Keble, Newman nor Pusey was particularly concerned about matters of ceremonial. Their preoccupation was far more concentrated on sacramental principle and the sacramental nature of the Church. The concern for reverence in prayer which was characteristic of the old high churchmen and the emphasis of the Oxford leaders on the sacramental principle, however, had important implications for the expression of those concerns in external devotion. Those implications were soon taken up by early disciples, especially those who had pastoral responsibility and wanted to redeem the accepted norms from an arid formalism.

Cambridge was a more important focus for these concerns than Oxford. In 1839 the Cambridge Camden Society was founded with the goal of reforming the architectural design of churches. The church building was to be a place of worship rather than a place of assembly for listening to a sermon. We have already observed how the Romantic spirit awakened a nostalgia for the medieval world which led to the lifting up of the Gothic religious spirit, and consequently its theology and piety, as the only truly appropriate Christian norm. Not only

17

should the building conform to the Gothic ideal, but the liturgical actions which take place in it should give expression to its implicit theology. This was the principle upon which the Camden Society based its work. Its object was 'to promote the study of Ecclesiastical Architecture and Antiquities, and the restoration of mutilated Architectural remains'. Its further goal was the restoration of norms for right worship.

The members of the Cambridge Camden Society were concerned with what they called 'ecclesiology', but not in the sense in which the word is ordinarily used today. 'Ecclesiology' was the science of church architecture, or more broadly, the science of Christian aesthetics. The members of the Society, and above all the editors of their publication *The Ecclesiologist*, fostered the idea not merely of the superiority of Gothic architecture in general for the design of churches, but more specifically that type of architecture known as 'pointed' or 'decorated', that is, the characteristic style of the century between 1260 and 1360: 'in pointed architecture Christian symbolism has found its most adequate exponent'.[1] The question was for them one not merely of design but of expressive integration with sound theology: 'Pointed Architecture seems to be so true a correlative to Christian doctrine, that we cannot suppose . . . that any future style will be discovered, in which the Pointed spirit shall not predominate.'[2] This attitude applied not only to the restoration of old buildings but also to the construction of new ones: 'It would be difficult to assign any reason why ancient churches should not be exactly copied as models for new ones.'[3]

The underlying issue here is not, of course, merely the question of a favoured design for church architecture. It is the much larger question of looking to the past to find definitive models for the life of the Church today, be it in architecture, liturgy, music, or doctrine. It is the familiar problem of looking back to a 'golden age' which sets forth the ideal from which later generations have strayed. For the members of the Cambridge Camden Society, this led to an uncritical bias for the centuries prior to the Reformation

18

as the standard for Christian theology and practice. When the Cambridge Ecclesiologists were criticized as sharing the Romanist sympathies of the Tractarian movement, at least one writer recognized that the issue was, as we have seen, part of the wider cultural picture: 'this general transition of taste is altogether a much larger matter; [it] belongs to the spirit of the age, not to . . . the Tractarian portion of the Establishment.'[4]

The principles propagated by the Society did not go uncriticized by some of their contemporaries: 'It is utterly preposterous to assert . . . that a style of architecture is exclusively christian and catholic which was not introduced till twelve long ages of Christianity had lapsed, and with which not more than half of Christendom was ever acquainted.'[5] Yet the Society asserted precisely that, and their influence was extraordinary. In retrospect we see, of course, that their idealization of the architecture of the fourteenth century led, in numerous restoration projects, to the destruction of much that was authentically medieval because it did not conform to the favoured model. As Sir Kenneth Clark has pointed out, 'It would be interesting to know if the Camden Society destroyed as much medieval architecture as Cromwell. If not it was from lack of funds.'[6]

Although the Cambridge Camden Society disclaimed theological and ritualistic concerns, the implications of their principles extended far beyond the narrowly architectural. In 1843 John Mason Neale, a founding member of the Society, wrote: 'I am sure that once churches are built or restored to be equal to those of older times . . . the poverty of our present vestments will become intolerable.'[7] The externals associated with medieval Catholic worship were increasingly seen as the sign of the recovery of Catholic doctrine, rather statically (if somewhat eclectically) based upon medieval models. A publication of the period, *The Christian Remembrancer*, challenged the Society in 1842 in the following words: 'Let then our architectural antiquarians, who would have us build after the manner of the thirteenth and fourteenth centuries, prove to us that we ought to worship after the manner of those centuries.' But that was indeed the ideal which the principles of the Society implied.

The architectural model which was fostered by the Cambridge Camden Society created a set of expectations about the nature of liturgical norms which the Church in England had not experienced as characteristic since the sixteenth century. The restoration of churches and the building of new ones according to the fostered model thus created a movement toward a recovery of medieval ritual as the authentically Catholic expression of liturgical prayer. On the one hand, this led to the fulfilment of the familiar apprehension about a pro-Roman sympathy. Those who were concerned about the reintroduction of Catholic ritual practices into Anglican use had little alternative except to look towards Rome, either by restoring the liturgical customs of the medieval period or by looking to contemporary Roman custom as the currently official standard for the celebration of the medieval liturgical practices. In either case, the underlying problem was a kind of liturgical antiquarianism which took the medieval ritual patterns to be normative. What this implied was a static concept of the Church in which one period offered the unquestionable model for all aspects of liturgical and sacramental practice.

3 Models for the Church

The first significant impact of the ideas which came to be associated with the Oxford Movement was effected through the publication of a long series of documents which were called Tracts for the Times. The general teaching of the movement is by no means limited, however, to the often narrow and polarized views put forward in the Tracts. The posture of the Tracts is defensive: they are concerned with the reaffirmation of the Church's apostolic origins and authority within a society in which the writers feel these aspects of the Church have been, at the very least, obscured. The appeal of the Tracts again and again is to 'the Primitive Church', which is the idealized model upon which the Tracts base their claims. The claims often manifest a shrill or rigid character, which is perhaps to be expected of writers who are convinced that the present state of the Church is intolerable. They are sounding an alarm.

As the Ecclesiologists held out an architectural ideal based upon the model of the late thirteenth and early fourteenth centuries, the writers of the Tracts, on the other hand, proposed the model which they saw reflected in the writings of the early Fathers. It is not surprising to find that much space is given in the Tracts to the direct quotation of patristic sources in support of the particular question in discussion. Although the idealized periods are not the same, the basic attitude is common to the groups both at Oxford and at Cambridge, namely, that an earlier golden age is looked to as a model — as a static model — for what the contemporary Church is to be.

For nineteenth-century theology in general, at least so

far as we can judge from the approach taken in writings on the subject, the area of liturgy and sacraments is not seen as directly connected to the understanding of the Church. Ancient liturgies are seen as documents of primitive doctrine and discipline, and certainly the primitive forms are held up in the Tracts as the models for the liturgy today. But the Tracts, like other nineteenth-century writings, do not relate liturgy and sacraments to the Church's essentially corporate nature. (In fact, this link is one of the most significant contributions of the developments in sacramental theology in our own century, and will be more fully explored in the second part of this book.) The general approach of the Tracts is to see the sacraments as instruments of grace to the believer, thus permitting an extremely individualized sacramental piety within the context of a static model of the Church.

Thus, to place a discussion of the sacraments and the liturgy in relation to an analysis of the understanding of the Church would probably have struck theological writers of the nineteenth century, including the authors of the Tracts, as rather odd. Yet the nostalgia for earlier Christian models which we have noted in regard to doctrine, discipline, liturgical rites and architectural styles is itself a sign of the underlying mutuality of all these matters within the general framework of the Church's self-understanding. Whereas the static models are rightly remembered as characteristic of the ideals of both the Oxford and Cambridge Movements, they were the starting point for further reflection and for ideas which have come into their fullness in the twentieth century. It is in this sense that it is unjust to attribute only the narrow and polemical assertions of the Tracts to the Oxford Movement, because the movement also bore very different fruit in, for example, various of the Anglican sermons of John Henry Newman. Our discussion of the characteristic ecclesiology of the Oxford Movement will then also involve a view of the fresh stream which arose from it.

THE CHURCH: STATIC OR DYNAMIC?

In his study of the Oxford Movement entitled *The Anglican Revival*, the Swedish scholar Yngve Brilioth focuses a significant part of his analysis of the teaching of the movement on what he labels 'the static view of the Church'. Since this analysis bears in important ways upon the Tractarian understanding of liturgy and sacraments, it is appropriate to explore here the principal aspects of Brilioth's discussion. Although, as we have observed, nineteenth-century theological writers did not see strong links between the doctrine of the Church and sacramental theology, the two areas are inevitably mutually interdependent. To the degree that Brilioth's analysis of the 'static Church' concept is justified, we may expect to find it exercising a decisive influence upon the area of liturgical/sacramental theology, even when that influence is not fully articulated.

The early Tracts for the Times lifted up from the attitudes common to the old high church tradition one concept which became the key to the ecclesiastical system which they taught. That concept was the idea of Apostolic Succession. Upon this concept the writers placed as upon an essential foundation the issues of the Catholicity of the Church of England, the validity of its sacraments, and the integrity of its doctrine. The appeal was to an unbroken continuity with the Church of the Apostles, an appeal which had been characteristic of Anglicanism since the very earliest years of the English Reformation. The idea that Christ had given authority to his Apostles who had in turn given over that authority to their successors was thus a well-established idea, firmly rooted in the teaching of numerous Anglican writers.[8] The principle of Apostolic Succession, however, not only gained a new vitality in the Tracts, but also acquired a narrowness which is foreign to the spirit of the writers to whom the Tracts gave reference.

The old high Anglicanism had never seen the episcopate as so essential to the Church that those traditions without it were thereby 'unchurched'. Rather the episcopate was seen prior to 1833 by those who most esteemed it as an aspect of the authority inherited from the ancient and undivided Church. One might note, for example, the views expressed by William Beveridge (1637–1708), an important exponent of the old high churchmanship, in his sermon on 'Christ's Presence with His Ministers'.[9] Beveridge says that 'the Apostles, being thus ordained and instructed by Our Lord, took special care to transfer the same Spirit to others which they had received from Him. . . . For the whole care of the Church being committed unto them, they had power to constitute what officers they thought fit under them. But still they did it by laying their hands upon them and so communicating of the same Spirit unto them, which they had received from Christ.' The clear emphasis in Beveridge's sermon is upon the work of the Holy Spirit in the Church. The agent of authority is the Spirit who conveys that authority in the ordination rite, and who thus ensures that each generation of the Church carries the mark of apostolicity which has characterized it since its origin. The efficacy of any ecclesiastical office, Beveridge writes, 'depends altogether upon the Spirit of God'. The question of legitimate ministry is clearly a concern for the succession of this Spirit-filled ministration in which Christ is always present. There can be no doubt that Beveridge identifies this succession with that of the bishops from Christ's time to his own. But it is not conceived mechanically. The episcopate is the sign of an organic dynamic of the Church's life in which the Holy Spirit is seen as the primary agent. The danger to be seen in separation from a church with the Apostolic Succession lies in the separation from the assured sign of the Spirit's guidance. Among the writers of the Tracts, this seed idea took root and flourished as an exclusive and determinative aspect of the Church's legitimacy.

The principle of Apostolic Succession is being used here simply as an introduction to the idea of the Church to which it is intimately related: that is, the static view of the Church as bound to the norms established authoritatively in the earliest Christian centuries. Apostolic Succession in its relation to the general views on holy orders and to consequent ecumenical issues will be explored in another volume of this series. Our primary concern here is not then an analysis of the Tractarian concept of ministry but rather the more fundamental question of the concept of the Church which lies behind it.

William Palmer (1803—85) of Worcester College, Oxford, who published his *Origines Liturgicae* in 1832 and was thus among the first writers to bring serious scholarship to the study of liturgical sources, was a firm defender of a very narrow understanding of Apostolic Succession. Although he remained rather removed from the leadership of the movement, his ideas were influential as, for example, in his authorship of the material upon which Newman based Tract 15, 'On the Apostolical Succession in the English Church', published in 1833. This brief tract is essentially a defence of the succession of bishops in the Church of England as being faithful to Christ's own institution. It is both anti-papalist and anti-nonconformist in being critical of the excessive claims of Rome and the illegitimacy of the nonconformist ministry. It is interesting to note that the tract concludes with a defence of Luther's break with Rome, saying that 'we are fully justified in maintaining that the conduct of those who defended the truth against the Romish party, even in opposition to their spiritual rulers, was worthy of great praise.' How, then, is the loss of the Apostolic Succession among Lutherans to be viewed? The tract says that 'it is impossible not to lament that they did not take the first opportunity to place themselves under orthodox Bishops of the Apostolical Succession'. At this early stage, the succession is certainly desirable but its absence does not seem to imply an essential defect.

Within a few years, Palmer's views on the subject achieved a much more rigid form. In 1838, he published *A Treatise on the Church of Christ*. With regard to its static conception of the Church, it must be regarded as proposing one of the narrowest interpretations of the authority of Christian ministry which has ever been

25

conceived, and is thus valuable as an indication of the understanding of the nature of the Church upon which this interpretation was based.

In his discussion of the Church as 'One, Holy, Catholic and Apostolic', Palmer places his discussion of the ministry under the last of these characteristics. Having earlier asserted that not all Christian denominations are part of the visible Church, Palmer goes on to tie the authentic Christian ministry to his view of Apostolic Succession. The divine commission for sacred office can only be given 'by means of ministers authorized to convey it to others'. He then goes on to define the clear restrictions upon the form through which this authorization takes place.

> The mode by which this commission was conveyed must always be essentially the *same*. Now, the apostolic mode of ordination, by which the apostles and their successors, the bishops of the universal church, sent forth the ministers of Jesus Christ, by imposition of hands and prayer — this mode *alone* has *always* existed in the church. For many ages popular elections were unheard of. The apostolic mode of ordination *alone* prevails in all ages, and among all nations. It is therefore evidently the external vocation instituted by God himself. If it be not so, if it be a mode of human invention, it could never have constituted ministers of Christ, and therefore the whole church would for many ages have been without true ministers; it would have been deficient in what is *essential* to the church of Christ, and therefore the catholic church must have *entirely failed*: a position which is directly and formally heretical.
>
> The great external sign of such a continuance of ordinations in any church, is derived from the legitimate succession of its chief pastors from the apostles; for it is morally certain, that wherever there has been this legitimate succession, the whole body of the clergy have been lawfully commissioned.[10]

26

The ecclesiology or concept of the Church which lies behind this passage is not one in which the dominant image of the Christian community is its formation through 'water and the Spirit', that is, through the rites of Christian initiation. The dominant image, rather, is that of a hierarchical ministerial structure whose authenticity is established through tactile succession in ordination. It is thus the true ministry which establishes the true Church, and any group of Christians in separation from that specific ministerial structure cannot be part of the visible Church of Jesus Christ. The Church is in this approach defined in terms of the ministry rather than in terms of Baptism. It is not surprising that the Anglicans who held this or a similar view maintained not merely a high view of ministerial authority but also what we would today recognize as a very inadequate view of the laity.

A further consequence of this emphasis upon the Apostolic Succession as the basis for an authentic ministry is found in the frequent assertion that the validity of the sacraments depends entirely upon their being administered only by bishops within the succession or by other clergy ordained by them. In Tract 74, which is a collection of materials from post-Reformation English writers concerning 'the Doctrine of the Apostolical Succession', we find it asserted that non-episcopal forms of ministry, 'men thus sending themselves, or sent by we know not whom', have no authority to administer the sacraments. It is not our intention to question the wisdom of the confiding of sacramental authority by the Church to its authorized ministers, but rather to indicate the danger in so narrow a restriction as we find here. In this context, the sacraments become virtually the possession of the clergy. They cease to be stewards of the sacraments on behalf of the Church, and become instead the primary agents in any sacramental action. Again, there is a question implied here as to the nature of the Church. In their concern for ministerial validity, the Tractarians lost a sense of the ecclesial foundation for every sacramental action. The use of 'ecclesial' in this context is a reference to the organic nature of the

27

Church as a sacramental communion of believers rather than the more familiar 'ecclesiastical' model identified with hierarchical authority, canon law and authorized liturgical rites. It is the whole Church which acts in, for example, the celebration of the Eucharist. The clergy receive specific authority for presiding in these actions through delegation from the Church at ordination, but that delegated authority must never be allowed to obscure the fact that the primary actors in a sacramental act are the whole assembly of the baptized people of God.

APOSTOLIC SUCCESSION OR APOSTOLICITY?

Why was this theory of Apostolic Succession of such crucial importance to the Oxford leaders? We have already observed the desperate situation of the Church during the first decades of the nineteenth century. Through a long process it had come to be viewed and experienced as nothing more than a department of state, an organizational convenience for dealing with religious matters in society. The Tractarians recognized the urgent need for finding a secure foundation for their view of the Church as a divinely established institution whose authority rested only upon Jesus Christ by direct delegation to his apostles and their successors. Only in this way could the Church be secured against the assaults of the liberal secularism of the time. The principle of Apostolic Succession was the key to their claims for the independence of the Church, but the critical situation of the English Church led the Tractarians to isolate one aspect of the meaning of Apostolic Succession from the rich complex of ideas in which its full meaning is manifested.

When the creeds confess the Church to be 'apostolic', it is an assertion that the Church in every age lives in continuity with the Church of the Apostles and their proclamation. The whole of that continuity involves, certainly, the transmission of ministerial authority from one generation to the next through the laying on of hands. But continuity also involves other aspects of apostolicity:

28

witness to the apostolic faith and its proclamation, engagement in apostolic service to those in need, unity among the local churches, and faithfulness in the celebration of Baptism and Eucharist. Nothing less than this full complex of apostolic faith and practice is adequate to what may be truly called the apostolic tradition. Tragically, the Oxford leaders did not perceive the full meaning of the apostolicity which they claimed for the Church, and separated the aspect of tactile succession from the context which gave it meaning. They thus opened the door within Anglicanism to the possibility of a Catholic caricature of the Church in which holy order can exist in its own validity apart from the life of the Church as a whole. In due course, Apostolic Succession was restored to the wider framework of its meaning, but as an issue it left an indelible mark upon the Oxford Movement and its heritage. Even in current ecumenical dialogue there is a tendency among the contemporary heirs of Tractarianism to isolate the question of the validity of ordination through Apostolic Succession from other equally significant aspects of the Church's life.

From the perspective of our own time, there is a certain naive character to the assertions of the Tracts concerning Apostolic Succession. Perhaps it is the approach to the Bible which is most striking. We are reminded how much these writings reflect a period when the critical study of scripture was in its earliest stages. Their authors were generally opposed to the critical method in any case. We find oversimplified explanations of what more recent scholarship has revealed to be complex and subtle issues, as, for example, the easy identification of the Apostles as the first bishops and the presumption of an early threefold structuring of church order which actually took many decades to evolve. Such opinions were not new in Anglicanism, of course, for already in his preface to the Ordinal of 1550 Archbishop Thomas Cranmer had stated that 'It is evident unto all men, diligently reading Holy Scripture and ancient Authors, that from the Apostles' time there have been these Orders of Ministers in Christ's Church — Bishops, Priests, and Deacons.' Yet the Tractarians accepted this inherited view and built upon it a concept of Apostolic Succession which makes untenable historical claims, as when Newman wrote in Tract 7 that 'Every link in the chain is known, from St. Peter to our present Metropolitans'. What we see here is an emphasis upon the tactile link between episcopal consecrators and the successors whom they consecrate. We sense an almost mechanistic understanding of succession.

The documents of the primitive Church indicate that the emphasis was rather to be found in the succession of occupants of the episcopal chair in a specific Christian community. This view sees the episcopal office in an organic relation with the ongoing life of the local church, not as a self-contained and self-authenticating basis for ecclesiastical validity. Such an organic model of the Church, however, does not accord with the spirit of the Tracts. Their ideal is the primitive model in the idealized form in which they conceived it. It is thus a static model, a model which the contemporary Church is required to duplicate in all essential aspects, and to which it is linked through Apostolic Succession. That task, of course, was, in the view of the Tracts, most adequately fulfilled by the Church of England, providentially preserved from the errors of Rome on the one hand and the disorganization of the nonconformists on the other. The world of the Tracts is thus a very small world indeed.

4   The Sacramentality of the Church

It was suggested earlier that the theological views associated with the Oxford Movement should not be limited to the polemical positions taken by the writers of the Tracts for the Times. Their purpose in the Tracts was to sound an alarm to a moribund Church. They wanted to awaken the members of the Church to an awareness of its true identity. We may by way of contrast, for example, consider the theological stance of Newman in his sermons on the nature of the Church. Whereas the Apostolic Succession left so strong a mark upon Newman's Tracts as well as those of other writers, the theme plays a rather minor role in the sermons and is referred to primarily as a providential sign of God's care for his Church. In the sermons Newman seems more concerned with reflection on the nature of the Church than with divisive argument.

Although Newman does not explicitly refer to the Church as a sacrament of Christ, he remains but one step short of that assertion. This is an important insight into the nature of the Church which, as we shall see later, comes to fruition in the sacramental theology of the twentieth century. Here we find a fresh perception which perhaps owes its origins to the rediscovery of the sacramental principle by the Tractarians. In his reflection on the nature of a sacrament, Newman was led to a further step, to at least the suggestion that particular sacramental actions refer in the end to an underlying sacramentality which inheres in the Body of Christ itself.

Such an idea is implied in Newman's sermon 'The Church Visible and Invisible'. Early in the sermon, Newman says that 'The word Church, applied to the body of

Christians in this world, means but one thing in Scripture, a visible body invested with invisible privileges.' This definition echoes, of course, the traditional definition of a sacrament as an outward sign of an invisible grace. Newman's purpose is to oppose any suggestion that the invisible Church of the elect of God is not to be identified with the visible Church, as though the latter were simply a human institution separated from any essential relation to God's saving work. In order to emphasize their inter-dependence, Newman notes that 'It is allowable to speak of the Visible and of the Invisible Church, as two sides of one and the same thing, separated by our minds only, not in reality.' Newman is saying that the visible, institutional Church bears an essential relation to God's purpose, that it is itself an instrument of grace. He is answering the critics of the institutional Church who are able to point to its sins and failures as an indication of its human rather than divine origin. That evil men are members of the visible Church is, it is proposed, a sign that grace is not at work in their lives. Newman responds by saying that 'we shall be nearer the truth, if, instead of saying "bad men cannot be members of the true Church," we word it, "bad men cannot be true members of the Church".' Newman thus acknowledges that there are baptized Christians who do not live up to their commitment, but the sin is their own and not a sign that the visible Church is not an instrument of God's grace. The Church, Newman writes, is 'that Holy House which Christ formed in order to be the treasury and channel of His grace to mankind, over which His Apostles presided at the first, and after them others whom they appointed'. The Church then, in Newman's thought, itself bears the nature of a sacrament.

In another sermon, 'The Visible Church an Encourage-ment to Faith', Newman gives his understanding of how the invisible Church of all God's elect people is related to the visible institutional Church. He writes, 'The Visible Church of God is that one only company which Christians know as yet; it was set up at Pentecost, with the Apostles for founders, their successors for rulers, and all professing

32

Christian people for members. In this Visible Church the Church Invisible is gradually moulded and matured.' This process is the work of the Holy Spirit in each individual believer, but it is not a work merely of individual sanctification. As for the sanctification of individual believers, 'all these blessed fulfilments of God's grace are as yet but parts of the Visible Church; they grow from it; they depend upon it.' The visible Church may not then, in Newman's thought, be seen merely as a source for individual sanctification, because all of the Spirit's work is ultimately ordered to the corporate life of the visible body in which the lives of both the committed and the lax are inseparably joined.

This union of the worthy with the unworthy is also reflected in the succession of bishops. In the same sermon, Newman affirms the apostolic rooting of the Church: Christ 'set it up on the foundation of His Twelve Apostles'. He affirms the Apostolic Succession: 'Every Bishop of the Church whom we behold, is a lineal descendent of St. Peter and St. Paul after the order of a spiritual birth.' The bishops have, he writes, 'received by succession of hands the power first given to the Apostles and now to us'. Yet Newman acknowledges that even this fundamental aspect of the Church's life also bears the mark of fallibility. 'True it is,' he writes, 'that at various times the Bishops have forgotten their high rank and acted unworthily of it,' have 'lived to this world, have fancied themselves of this world, have thought their office secular and civil.' Yet, in spite of these failures, Christ has remained faithful to his Church and the ministry which he established: 'He said, He would be with His Church: He has continued it alive to this day. He has continued the line of His Apostles onwards through every age and all troubles and perils of the world.' Newman's view of the Church thus incorporates an honest awareness of human weakness, and sees it as a sign of Christ's continued faithfulness to the visible Church which he founded. Human sin, for Newman, cannot be the basis for a denial of the Church's divine origin.

It is in the structures of the visible Church that God's

elect find the sustenance of the life of faith. Newman writes that

> the true elect of God . . . are scattered about amid the leaves of that Mystical Vine which is seen, and receive their nurture from its trunks and branches. They live on its Sacraments and Ministry; they gain light and salvation from its rites and ordinances; they communicate with each other through it; they obey its rulers; they walk together with its members; they do not dare to judge of this man or that man, on their right hand or their left, whether or not he is absolutely of the number of those who shall be saved; they accept all as their brethren in Christ, as partakers of the same general promises, who have not openly cast off Christ, — as really brethren, till death comes, as those who fulfil their calling most strictly.[11]

Newman's view of the Church is thus as an instrument of God incorporating all the baptized, and consequently establishing the framework for the instrumentality of redemption which is effected in its fundamental common acts, Baptism and Eucharist. God's hidden work of justification is expressed through these external actions; their sacramentality is a mirror to the fundamental sacramentality of the Church itself. The sanctification which is the fruit of this work of God is for Newman, as we observed earlier, the explicit work of the Holy Spirit. The Body of Christ is the dwelling place of the Spirit, who is the divine energy of its sanctifying work.

We find in Newman's preaching a dynamic concept of the Church which reaches far beyond the rigidities of the ecclesiology of the Tracts, with their often unbalanced emphasis upon Apostolic Succession. Certainly the sermons speak of the importance of the Apostles and the leaders who succeeded them, but this concern for the ordained ministry is held in balance, placed within a wider framework of sacramentality which inheres in the Church as a whole, and which gives more adequate space to the work

34

of God throughout the whole life of the Body. Newman's purpose is to show that the institutional Church is not merely a humanly sustained social organism, but that it is integral to God's way of working in the world, that it is an instrument of grace. In this perspective, of course, the particular sacraments assume a decisive importance for the life of faith.

THE CHURCH AS INSTRUMENT OF GRACE

The doctrine of the Church which developed among the leaders of the Oxford Movement was, as we have observed, shaped by the cultural and ecclesiastical situation of the time. The idea of the sacramentality of the Church ran counter to the rationalism which had exerted so great an influence upon the Church of England. The emphasis upon the divine institution of the episcopate was, for the Tractarians, a means of affirming the sacramental foundation of the Church. The question of the apostolic ministry was the issue to which the Tractarians gave their early and most intense attention. That question, however, implied some larger issues about the nature of the Church.

Anglicanism from Richard Hooker onward had taken a stand for the Church as a visible society in opposition to the common reformed concept of the invisible Church. Hooker's concern was for the rights of the Church as a visible society to order its own life and not, as the Puritans taught, to implement only those matters in both worship and practice which are clearly authorized by scripture. It was in this regard that Hooker clearly and definitively set the limits of the influence of Calvinism upon the Church of England. Newman's emphasis upon the visible Church adds a further dimension to the foundational views of Hooker, the teaching of both men being shaped by the situation which they addressed. Although at times Newman developed an idea which had first appeared in the work of another, his writings on the doctrine of the Church are the most original to come out of the movement, and are indeed prophetic of much of the ecclesiological writing of our century. For this reason, in a brief study of this kind, we shall draw primarily upon Newman's teaching, especially as found in certain of his sermons. For Newman the visible nature of the Church implies an essential visibility in the acts which characterize its social existence. In this perspective, the sacraments are not ancillary to faith, but are its visible articulations.

This outward aspect of the Church is not merely the means of its historical link in human history with the Apostolic Church; it is the means used by the Holy Spirit in his present and continuing activity within the Church. 'The Holy Spirit,' Newman writes, 'has vouchsafed to take up His abode in the Church, and the Church will ever bear, on its front, the visible signs of its hidden privilege.'[12] Or, as he says elsewhere, the Church's 'Sacraments are the Instruments which the Holy Ghost uses.'[13] The work of the Spirit to convert and sanctify Christians is integral to the visible nature of the Church as a divine society in human history.

God did not, in Newman's view, simply *originate* the Church, as the deists of the eighteenth century would have it, but continues to live in it, and to sanctify mankind through its instrumentality. It is a 'means in the hands of God'. Through it the gifts of the Holy Spirit are imparted. It is thus through membership in the Church that persons are enabled to participate in these gifts. The Christian assembly is the recipient of the gifts in a primary sense. Newman says that Christ 'has lodged His blessings in the body collectively to oblige them to meet *together* if they would gain grace each for himself. The body is the first thing and each member in particular the second. The body is not made up of individual Christians, but each Christian has been made such in his turn by being *taken into the body*.'[14]

In principle, this quotation indicates a strong opposition on Newman's part to religious individualism. He is asserting the ecclesial or corporate nature of grace. Such a view stands radically against the privatization of religious experience which so characterized pietism and which left a significant mark upon the various churches. To a great extent, nineteenth-century piety was strongly individualistic even within the liturgical traditions. The individualism of the Romantic movement simply added a further dimension to what was already a characteristic of common religious views. This wider context, both cultural and religious, inhibited the realization of Newman's views in this regard. From our present perspective, his insistence upon the ecclesial nature of grace was a prophetic insight into a basic aspect of the sacramental system which we have only begun in our own time to integrate into the practical piety of the Church. It is an insight with far-reaching implications for the meaning of sacraments in the Church's life.

As the sacramental nature of the Church was emphasized, so the results of that sacramentality came to be sought. If the sacraments are effective instruments of God's grace, then their power in the lives of believers is expected to be manifest. The goal of God's grace is transformation, the building up of the Body of Christ. The sacraments are the means by which God becomes directly present and active in the members of the Church. The holiness which the Creed ascribes to the Church is through Baptism extended to its individual members. Thus the justification by faith of individual believers is, for Newman, directly linked to the instrumentality of grace effected by God through the Church and its sacraments. In this sense, the whole of the Church's life is a kind of extension of what God has done in Christ. In other words, the Church is an extension of the Incarnation, its purpose being totally united with the act of God in Christ for the salvation of the world. Christ is thus the foundation sacrament from which the sacramental nature of the Church is derived. The work of the Holy Spirit through the sacraments is to effect that transformation to new life which is offered through the death and resurrection of Jesus. This work of the Spirit continues into every successive generation as the benefits of Christ's self-offering are communicated to the believing community through the instrumentality of sacramental grace.

Newman taught that the Incarnation, the 'mediatorial plan of salvation . . . is not in itself new or unusual, and displayed for the first time in the Christian system, but one which [God] has made use of every where and in every age for the preservation and benefit of the human race.' The sacramental system which Newman identifies with this 'mediatorial plan of salvation' is not limited to Christianity but is rather the fundamental model of God's way of working in his world because of the divine transcendence. In the same sermon Newman writes,

> God is at a distance from our senses and direct apprehension; according to the course of nature He can have no immediate communication with us. . . . All He does for us and gives us is through the instrumentality, *or the mediation* of others. . . . The Christian Church itself is one most important mediator between God and the world — being intended to be the means of proclaiming and impressing the truth on men's hearts and converting them from sin to holiness. It receives the gifts of the Holy Spirit from God, and by sacraments and ordinances, by prayers, by preaching, by establishments for education, it conveys them to the world at large.[15]

This passage is of enormous significance, not only in its assertion about the instrumentality of the sacraments, but also in placing that instrumentality in the context of God's abiding way with mankind. Incarnation/mediation/sacrament are not one 'method' of religion among others; they are the only foundation for human communication with the Holy One. The Church is not an arbitrary religious society; it is itself the fundamental sign of God's unique way of intercourse with the world. It is God's agent in the world, not, by implication, merely for the spiritual nurture of the Christian believers, but ultimately for the life of the whole world. What Newman is claiming here is that the Church is far more than merely a source of sacramental grace for persons disposed to that type of Christianity, but is the instrument on earth by which God continues the work of the Incarnation. Through the Church, Christ continues his ministry of mediation, and the sacraments are the effective means by which that mediation is expressed. The Incarnation is not merely a past event in history; God is eternally incarnate in the ongoing life of the Body of Christ.

It is easy to see how such a doctrine of Church and sacraments stood in opposition to the rationalism which had dominated the English Church for so long and which saw external practices as being, at best, unrelated in any essential way to primary religious matters. The very idea of a mediatorial Church was inimical to the liberal views of the period. Thomas Arnold (1795–1842) reflected the characteristic response of this school in his *Fragment on the Church*, where he speaks of a religion of reason based upon faith which 'assures us of the utter incapability of any outward bodily action to produce in us an inward spiritual effect'. Liberal Anglicanism emphasized the primacy of inward religion and its effect upon man's moral nature. In such a view, sacraments as external instruments of grace had no place, and similarly the whole idea of a sacramental Church was foreign to liberal convictions.

The Evangelicals also were unsympathetic to the sacramental views of the Tractarians. For the Evangelicals, the sacraments and other external aspects of religious practice were merely tokens of the gifts of God which were communicated to the believer by the Holy Spirit. This communication was accomplished directly to the inner soul without any intermediary. The critical matter which separated the Evangelicals from the Tractarians was the interpretation of justification by faith alone. How could Christian sacramental practice be understood in such a way that this primary doctrine of the Reformation would not be invalidated? For the Evangelicals the sacraments could not be an effective means of grace if justification was to rest uniquely upon the work of God in Christ. This justification was a *spiritual* gift, the invisible work of the Holy Spirit, who is the one who forms the invisible Church of true believers. In this respect, the Evangelicals were as critical in their own way of the established Church as were the Tractarians, but whereas the latter summoned the visible Church to the implications of its divine origin, the former were as content as the Liberals to ascribe to the visible Church no supernatural authority and to see it as a dimension of the state.

For both the Liberals and the Evangelicals, religious practice focused in a strong individualism. The emphasis upon reason on the one hand and feeling on the other did not in either case lead to a valuing of the corporate aspect of Christianity. It is, as we have seen, precisely from this latter foundation that the Tractarians gave their response. In the doctrine of the Church they found a framework for uniting the internal and the external dimensions of Christian faith. Religious individualism combined with an excessive emphasis upon the rational aspects of faith, or, on the other hand, upon a spiritualized understanding of religious experience, lost sight of the primacy of the role of the Church in Christianity. The Church, for the Tractarians, was the instrument of God for the unity of mankind in Christ. Another of the Oxford writers, Robert Wilberforce (1802–57), developed this idea in a work first published in 1848.

> Our union with the manhood of Christ, or our participation in His Presence, is brought about in our union with the Church, which is His body mystical. It is not that one of these is a means or channel through which we approach the other, but that since the two processes are identical it is impossible to divide them. For that which joins men to Christ's mystical body the Church, is their union with His man's nature; and their means of union with His man's nature is bestowed in His Church or body mystical. This will become more evident, when it is shown that the Sacraments, which are the means of binding us to the mystical body of Christ, derive their efficacy from the influence of His body natural. . . . By the

mystical body of Christ, is meant the whole family of those who by the Holy Ghost are united in Church ordinances to His man's nature. Our real union with each is what gives us a part in the other.[16]

In other words, the external sacraments are integral to God's plan; they are the divinely appointed means through which we are promised his grace and blessing. But these sacraments are never acts of private piety; they always refer to the underlying sacramentality of the Church from which they receive their power and meaning. The Church is itself the primary instrument of grace.

5 Baptism and Eucharist

The concept of the sacramentality of the Church which was taught by Newman and the other Tractarians implied, of course, a strong emphasis upon the role of the individual sacraments in the Christian life. Most of this material concerns Baptism and the Eucharist. Aside from substantial attention addressed to the legitimation of the ordained ministry through the laying on of hands by bishops in the Apostolic Succession, there is very little attention given to the so-called lesser sacraments. In fact, we find in earlier Tracts, a rejection of the Roman system of seven sacraments.[17] Later, in Tract 90, in his discussion of Article XXV, Newman allows that they may be seven in number as long as it is acknowledged that Baptism and the Eucharist hold a pre-eminent rank.

Newman asserts that in Anglicanism the number of the sacraments is not strictly determined, but rather that the word may be applied generally to any 'outward sign of an inward grace'. Baptism and Eucharist have a special importance as 'generally necessary to salvation', but following upon the teaching of St Augustine quoted in one of the Homilies, Newman suggests that many ordinances may be called sacraments if they conform to the essential meaning as outward signs of the promises of God. The idea of innumerable sacraments which yet do not rival the primacy of Baptism and Eucharist is a concept also found in the sacramental writings of Eastern Orthodox theologians of the twentieth century.

In the extensive material on Baptism and Eucharist which we find in the Tracts, one essential concern emerges as dominant, a concern which derives from the theology of the Church which was fundamental to the entire Tractarian system. Newman raises the issue succinctly in the discussion of Article XXV which was referred to above. Speaking to the questioned sacramentality of Confirmation, Penance, Orders, Matrimony, and Extreme Unction, Newman says, 'They are not sacraments in *any* sense, *unless* the Church has the power of dispensing grace through rites of its own appointment, or is endued with the gift of blessing and hallowing the "rites or ceremonies" which, according to the twentieth article, it "hath power to decree". But we may well believe that the Church has this gift.' For Newman the question of the number of the sacraments is linked to a far more basic issue, the divine authority given to the Church as an effective instrument of grace. It is useless to engage in debates about the number of the sacraments or their comparative importance if it has not first been acknowledged that the Church is a sacramental society whose rites bear the reality of what they signify. Newman recognized that arguments about two sacraments being instituted by Christ as contrasted with some other category of sacramental acts were vain if there was not an initial acknowledgement of the real instrumentality of any such actions because they are the appointed signs of divine grace and power, and not merely appendages to faith.

In his preface to the second volume of the Tracts, Newman indicates that Anglican theology had been too much influenced by those whom he characterizes as 'Puritan or Latitudinarian', that is, the Evangelicals and the Liberals. As a consequence, he writes,

we have almost embraced the doctrine that God conveys grace only through the instrumentality of the mental energies, that is, through faith, prayer, active spiritual contemplation, or (what is commonly called) communion with God, in contradiction to the primitive view according to which the Church and her Sacraments are the ordained and direct visible means of conveying to the soul what is itself supernatural and unseen.[18]

Newman's purpose is to oppose any form of sacramental receptionism in which 'the strong wish, or moral worth, of the individual could create in the outward ceremony a virtue which it had not received from above'.

It was a critical concern for the Tractarians in their writings on the sacraments to contradict, in Newman's words, the false rationalism which had 'infected a large mass of men in our communion', and which engendered 'a slowness to believe the possibility of God's having literally blessed ordinances with invisible power'. Yet further, the Tractarians were also anxious to demonstrate what they saw to be the integral relation between sacraments and faith. Whereas for the Evangelicals faith involved an essentially interior nurturing by the Holy Spirit, the Tractarians understood faith as the requisite precondition on the human side for the fruitful reception of the grace initiated by God through the instrumentality of the sacraments. It is God only who makes a sacrament a means of grace; this is in no way dependent upon 'the strong wish or moral worth of the individual'. It is not a merely subjective, but an *objective* reality, encompassing both God's initiative act and the subjective response.

This position was given significant expression in Tract 67, Pusey's 'Scriptural Views of Holy Baptism', which established the author as one of the leaders of the Oxford Movement. On the relation of faith to the sacraments, Pusey writes:

> [Our Lord] places two conditions of salvation before us; one required on our part, the other promised on His; one a requisite *in* us, though His gift *in* us, the other His gift *to* us; Faith, whereby we desire to be healed, and his gift, whereby He healeth us. . . . It is not then for us to establish any comparison between the two conditions to which our Lord has here annexed salvation; they are plainly incommensurables; any quality in us can have no proportion to God's gift to us.[19]

Although faith is itself God's gift, Pusey was concerned that faith should not be separated from the gift of Baptism to which it is by divine ordinance united. Any idea of salvation by faith only, which reduced the sacramental sign to a secondary or superfluous status, was irreconcilable with his teaching on the instrumentality of the sacraments. As he wrote in the preface to Tract 67, 'The Blessed Sacraments then are a daily testimony to our faith: we are strengthened, we hold onwards: *how* we obtain our strength we can give to reason no account: suffice that we know *whence* it cometh.'

When we turn to a specific consideration of the sacraments of Baptism and Eucharist, we find, of course, many issues touched upon which it would lie beyond the limits of this book to examine. The major concerns in regard to both sacraments, however, are directly related to the question of sacramental instrumentality which was fundamental to the Tractarian doctrine of the Church.

BAPTISM

The dominant issue with respect to Baptism was the doctrine of baptismal regeneration. As indicated in its title, Pusey set out in Tract 67 to examine the teaching of scripture on the subject. Pusey held that scripture was quite clear in its support of baptismal regeneration, which he defined as 'the act by which God takes us out of our relation to Adam and makes us actual members of His Son'. Pusey saw the doctrine as grounded in the teaching of both Jesus and St Paul, but it is clear that for him the issue is rooted in the larger question of the reality of sacramental grace. If it is merely an outward form without any assured gift of God's grace, then obviously reliance upon it is a deadly illusion. But if Baptism is the instrument of the grace of regeneration, then it implies far-reaching consequences in the life of the baptized person. That Baptism as established in the Bible effects such a regeneration was for Pusey an indisputable matter of faith.

In Newman's sermon 'Regenerating Baptism' we find

the same understanding of the sacramental sign. It is the Holy Spirit, Newman writes, who admits individual members into the Church by means of Baptism. This incorporation involves regeneration as a necessary component. Newman centres his argument for baptismal regeneration on the question of the Baptism of infants, and emphasizes the instrumental role taken by the Spirit in his exposition of the text, 'By one Spirit are we all baptized into one Body' (1 Cor. 12:13). If, Newman asks, the sacred privilege of regeneration 'is not given to them in Baptism, why, it may be asked, should Baptism be administered to them at all?' The practice of the Baptism of infants must be based upon more than merely the Church's custom or else it makes a confusing contradiction to the expectation in adult candidates of repentance and faith as a precondition for Baptism.

Newman speaks next of the connection in scripture 'between Baptism and Divine grace', whereas the scriptural evidence for infant Baptism is far less clear.

> What right [Newman asks] have we to put asunder what God has united? especially since, on the other hand, the text cannot be found which plainly enjoins the Baptism of infants. If the doctrine and the practice are irreconcilable, — Baptismal Regeneration and Infant Baptism, — let the practice which is not written in Scripture, yield to the doctrine which is; and let us (if we can bear to do so) defraud infants of Baptism, not Baptism of its supernatural virtue. Let us go counter to Tradition rather than to Scripture.[20]

Newman's intention, of course, is not to oppose the practice of infant Baptism but rather to raise the question of the integrity of its meaning. In doing so, he shows the essentially sentimental and falsifying aspects of the practice if it is not supported by a strong theory of its meaning. Indiscriminate Baptism of infants continues in our own day to raise this question because it is either an empty form, or else, if it is the instrument of the grace of regeneration, it is a gift of grace conferred upon conditions which should affect the life-style of the whole family in living their baptismal promises.

Newman's concern for the *meaning* of Baptism leads inevitably to the characteristic Tractarian affirmation of the instrumentality of the sacraments, which 'are not mere outward signs, but (as it were) effluences of His grace developing themselves in external forms'. The external matter of the sacrament becomes the effective means of a true spiritual power.

> Thus in a true sense that water is not what it was before, but is gifted with new and spiritual qualities. Not as if its material substance were changed, which our eyes see, or as if any new nature were imparted to it, but that the lifegiving Spirit, who could make bread of stones, and sustain animal life on dust and ashes, applies the blood of Christ through it; or according to the doctrine of the text, that He, and not man, is the baptizer.[21]

The heart of the issue is that the liturgical act is not merely an external form but that it signifies and is the effective instrument of an action of God through the Church: 'Either Baptism is an instrument of the Holy Ghost, or it has no place in Christianity.' The liturgical acts are not to be looked upon in themselves, 'but as signs of [Christ's] presence and power'. Baptism then, is a sign of the same instrumentality which Newman ascribed to the Church itself in a yet more fundamental way, an instrumentality which permeates the entire sacramental system.

This understanding of Baptism was the source of direct conflict between the Tractarians and the Evangelicals because of its implications for the doctrine of justification by faith. For the Evangelicals, justification by faith was the cornerstone of Christianity. Tractarian teaching on the sacraments appeared to them to undermine the primacy of that doctrine. In his *Lectures on Justification*, Newman set forth what he saw as the integral relation between justification and Baptism. Faith, he wrote, is 'the internal instrument' and Baptism 'the external instrument' of justification.

> The instrumental power of Faith cannot interfere with the instrumental power of Baptism; because Faith is the *sole* justifier, not in contrast to all means and agencies whatever, (for it is not surely in contrast to our Lord's merits, or God's mercy,) but to all other *graces*. When, then, Faith is called the sole instrument, this means the sole *internal* instrument, not the sole instrument of any kind. There is nothing inconsistent, then, in Faith being the sole instrument of justification, and yet Baptism also the sole instrument, and that at the same time, because in distinct senses; an inward instrument in no way interfering with an outward instrument. Baptism might be the hand of the giver, and Faith the hand of the receiver.[22]

Baptism is thus the outward instrument of justification as faith is its inward instrument.

This view was, of course, opposed by the Evangelicals because they thought it implied that the sacrament can be efficacious without regard to the moral state of the recipient. For the Tractarians, the union of justification with Baptism was essential in order to avoid any suggestion that salvation might rest upon human merit rather than upon God's initiative. This concern was clearly complementary to Tractarian convictions about the instrumental efficacy of the sacraments; yet Newman would not have this instrumental efficacy isolated from the moral question. As he wrote in Lecture XI of the same series on justification, 'Moral rectitude without faith would be a soul without eyes; faith without it would be perception without appreciation; it cannot read the message of mercy, though it gaze ever so hard; it is said to do so, as the eye is said to read, but it does not of itself appreciate or obey it'. The life-style of the individual who has received Baptism is thus the test of whether the person has truly assimilated the divine gift, just as the mind may or may not assimilate what the eye has read. Faith and sacramental instrumentality are not contradictory, but are, in the deepest sense, complementary for Newman. Their fruitfulness depends in many ways upon the Church's and the individual's living out of the implications of God's gift; but human failure in this regard is a sign of sin and not of any defect in the gift itself.

THE EUCHARIST

Anglican theology of the Eucharist has always been characterized by a certain reserve in speaking about the nature of this primary expression of the unity of all the baptized in Christ. The tendency in general has been to say little rather than much, and the affirmations concerning the Eucharist which Anglican theologians have chosen to make have often involved the setting of distinctions from the explanations offered by theologians of both the Roman Catholic and the reformed traditions. There is an irenic tone in Anglicanism which seeks to affirm as much as possible the common ground between itself and other traditions in regard to the Eucharist, and yet an unwillingness to overdefine what is perceived essentially as a profound mystery.

Richard Hooker (1554?–1600) established a framework for the discussion of the Eucharist in Anglicanism in *The Laws of Ecclesiastical Polity*, where he wrote, 'Variety of judgements and opinions argueth obscurity in those things whereabout they differ. But that which all parts receive for truth, that which every one having sifted is by no one denied or doubted of, must needs be a matter of infallible certainty.' In regard to the Eucharist, he offers as the Anglican teaching the following words as though spoken by Christ:

This hallowed food, through concurrence of divine power, is in verity and truth unto faithful receivers instrumentally a cause of that mystical participation, whereby, as I make Myself wholly theirs,

so I give them in hand an actual possession of all
such saving grace as My sacrificed Body can yield,
and as their souls do presently need, this is *to them
and in them* My Body.[23]

This statement offers a summary of the primary affirmations which Anglicanism has taught about the Eucharist:

1   that the physical elements remain material food;
2   that the elements are sanctified by divine power;
3   that the elements are instruments of the grace offered
    to mankind through the sacrifice of Christ;
4   that those who receive the elements in faith have
    access in them to this gift of saving grace.

Much is said, but also much is left undefined. The balance
in Hooker's definition may easily be overthrown by a
greater emphasis on one point or another. The reference to
'faithful receivers', for example, can easily become a basis
for a receptionist view if it is not held in tension with the
belief that the 'hallowed food' is 'instrumentally a cause'
of Christ's presence.

During the two centuries between Hooker and the
Tractarians, a wide range of views about the Eucharist was
voiced in Anglicanism, and the influence of rationalistic
Latitudinarianism had a strong impact upon the general
understanding of the Eucharist. The evidence suggests that
the anti-sacramental thrust of rationalism brought about a
loss of conviction among a significant number of Anglicans
that the Eucharist is an effective means of grace. A
memorialist or receptionist interpretation of the Eucharist
was common. Yet there remained a stream within
Anglicanism which held to a sacramental understanding of
the Eucharist throughout this long rationalist period. By
and large, this latter view may be identified with the old
high churchmen whom we considered earlier.

The focus of the pre-Tractarian high churchmanship was
found in the worship of the Church as expressed in the
Book of Common Prayer.[24] The chief writers of this

tradition saw the centre of that worship in the Eucharist, and regularly lamented its neglect. In their view, the eucharistic action involves the whole Church in the sacrifice of Christ in an intimate and direct way, and finds its completion in the act of communion which offers to all the faithful the benefits of Christ's death. Here the renewal of the covenant established on Calvary takes place in a way which permits believers to share in all the promises of the Gospel. In this perspective, the Eucharist and its act of communion, at that time sadly obscured as normative in the Roman rite, bear a direct relation to the meaning of Baptism. In communion the Body of Christ established through Baptism constitutes itself in each particular time and place.

The emphasis upon the doctrine of eucharistic sacrifice which we find in the writings of seventeenth-century high churchmen, and which was in general rejected by both Evangelicals and Latitudinarians, was in fact an insistence upon the instrumental link between the Eucharist and the sacrifice of Christ on Calvary. In this sense, the old high churchmen were, in their eucharistic piety, emphatically medieval, and not very different from Roman Catholics of their period except for certain differences in vocabulary, and their concern for the corporate nature of the liturgy. Jeremy Taylor is a rare exception in his association of the Eucharist with Christ's Resurrection, and in this anticipates the recovery of balance in eucharistic piety which is taking place in our own time. More common among the seventeenth-century writers is an affirmation of the relation of the liturgy to the corporate life of the Church, not as individuals but as a people. The liturgy is the act of a community, the Church, and its culmination is found in the eucharistic sacrifice and communion as an organic expression of their common life and common self-offering in Christ. The sacrifice of Christ is not an event locked in the past, but an eternal event in which each generation of the Church shares. These ideas were prophetic of developments in sacramental theology in the twentieth century, but were also the point of departure for the Tractarians.

TRACTARIANS AND THE EUCHARIST

Among the various Tractarian writings on the Eucharist, perhaps the most systematic views are presented in Robert Wilberforce's *The Doctrine of the Holy Eucharist*, published in 1853, only a year before the author became a Roman Catholic. Although they present a position very sympathetic to Roman Catholic eucharistic theology, they are important as a strong expression of an instrumental sacramental theology in reference to the Eucharist by an Anglican writer. As we noted earlier, there was a tendency in Anglican teaching on the Eucharist to avoid too precise a definition of the way in which the bread and wine become a means of the divine presence to believers. This meant, of course, that in regard especially to controversial areas in eucharistic theology there was a lack, and for some a frustrating lack, of clarity.[25]

In his book on the Eucharist, Wilberforce set out to address this situation by using not only the teaching of scripture in his exposition of the subject, but also that of numerous writers from approximately the first nine centuries, that is, prior to the separation of the Church in the West from that of the East, and prior to the first important eucharistic disputes. This was done, Wilberforce writes, due to the complexity of the subject because of certain ambiguities in scripture. The other references are thus used as a means of determining the Church's understanding of the scriptural foundation. In his introduction Wilberforce writes, 'The authority of Holy Scripture is first referred to, and its infallible decision set forth. When its meaning is disputed, reference is made to the Primitive Fathers, as providing the best means of settling the dispute.' The author's purpose, of course, was to show the legitimacy of his use of later writings to those who maintained that scripture is the only authority in all questions concerning Christian doctrine.

We have already considered the common Tractarian insistence upon the instrumentality of the sacraments as means of God's grace. Wilberforce writes that:

when we speak of sacraments as moral instruments, we are merely discriminating between the order of grace and the order of nature; we affirm that sacraments pertain to the first, whereas those things which are called physical instruments belong to the second. ... It is not meant, then, that sacraments are less certain in their effects than physical agents; nor yet that their *reality* depends upon those circumstances in their receivers, which are essential to their *utility*. But they are called moral instruments because they derive their validity from the immediate appointment of Him, who acts in common according to that law, which He has imposed upon the material creation; because they belong to the order of grace, and not to the order of nature. It is as a moral, and not a physical instrument then, that the outward form in the Holy Eucharist is the means of conveying the inward gift.[26]

The Eucharist is thus a supernatural instrument of Christ's presence. But how is this instrumentality effected? It is obvious that the spiritual power of the Eucharist is not found merely in the natural significance of the bread and wine for human nourishment. Rather, Wilberforce writes, the spiritual instrumentality of the Eucharist is seen in its sacramental union or identity with the presence of Christ. Not only does this view affirm a *real* presence, but it also respects the characteristic Anglican concern that the reality of the sign (the bread and wine) be not obscured or annihilated by the reality signified (the Body and Blood of Christ), an error which was frequently thought to be the meaning of transubstantiation, and which, for traditional Anglicanism, 'overthroweth the nature of a sacrament'. Wilberforce insists that a correct understanding of transubstantiation does not, in fact, fall into that error.

The emphasis placed by Wilberforce upon the instrumentality of the eucharistic sign is a firm application of the sacramental principle which had such fundamental importance for the Tractarians. His special contribution was to deal with this question in not only a systematic but also a creative way. His theory of sacramental union cut a secure line through eucharistic theories which failed to deal adequately with the subtle but necessary balance between both the reality and its sign.

The nature of the real presence of Christ in the Eucharist is a complementary aspect of the issue of sacramental instrumentality. The question remains that of a recurring affirmation among the Tractarians of God's use of physical/material means for the communication of grace, this seen simply as a carrying out of the implications of the doctrine of the Incarnation, with the Church understood as an extension of Christ's role as mediator. Christ is present in the sacramental acts of the Church because he wills to be thus present. This presence is *sacramental* in that it presumes faith for its discernment; it cannot be discerned by the senses. Yet it is also *real* and *objective* in that spiritual gifts are communicated through its instrumentality, not through subjective religious feelings, but through God's act.

The contribution of Wilberforce in this area of sacramental theology was of great significance in the evolution of views in Anglicanism. From the time of the Reformation there had been a preoccupation among Anglican writers to avoid any descriptive language concerning the Eucharist which might be interpreted in a 'carnal' sense. The long debate between Anglicans and Roman Catholics on this issue was grounded in a deep Anglican suspicion that the doctrine of transubstantiation involved such an implicitly idolatrous attitude. As a result of this tension, even high churchmen had resorted to ambiguous language in speaking of the real presence. Wilberforce's study of the Eucharist showed that it was possible to affirm belief in a true and objective presence which nevertheless respected the integrity and reality of the sacramental sign. In this regard, his approach marked the opening up of a renewed sacramental theology which has begun to exercise a critical importance in our own time.

6   The Influence of Roman Ritual Norms

The most common image of the impact of the Oxford Movement upon Anglican worship lies in the area of ritual enrichment and finally, for some, in the wholesale adoption of Roman Catholic rites and liturgical practices. From the perspective of today, with our deepening sense of the way in which a ritual tradition is the expression of a total ecclesial reality, that is, how a liturgy is rooted in the life of the church which celebrates it, this importation of Roman ritual into the liturgical life of Anglican parishes appears as an exceedingly odd phenomenon. To celebrate the Roman rite indicates, or certainly *should* indicate, that one shares totally in the Roman Catholic religious tradition, its identity, its customs, its papal polity, and finally in the sharing of the sacramental gifts centred in the communion of all the Christians in the world who share in all these aspects of the Roman tradition.

The importation of various elements of Roman ritual by post-Tractarian Anglo-Catholics is, however, an interesting phenomenon in the ecclesial situation of the nineteenth century. Certain liturgical customs were seen as 'Catholic' as contrasted with other customs which were not so. It was not a time of great historical knowledge as to the origin and development of such practices, and thus a certain objectivity as to their appropriateness for incorporation into Anglican liturgical practice was lacking. There was clearly no ecclesiastical authorization for these liturgical customs in the Anglican formularies. The question was, rather, that of utilizing liturgical customs which were associated with Catholicism. The problem, however, was that all of this was taking place under the powerful influence of the Romantic idealization of medieval Catholicism which, as we observed earlier, had led to a static model of Catholic faith and practice. It was thus possible, from our perspective rather naively, for Anglicans who wished to affirm the Catholic heritage of Anglicanism simply to adopt either antiquarian medieval English practices or, more conveniently, current Roman norms as the external expressions of the professed faith. This was a result of an oversimplified and quite narrow sense of the complexity of Catholicism in all these matters.

It has often been noted that the leading Tractarians, Keble, Newman and Pusey, were not concerned about the rubrical details and ceremonial niceties which became a characteristic preoccupation with those who looked to Roman legislation for the final word on liturgical matters. The liturgical heritage of the Tractarians was normally taken, as far as we can tell, from the customs of the old high church tradition. Although the high churchmen had a great love for the liturgy and would certainly have celebrated the rites of the Book of Common Prayer 'decently and in order', their use of outward ceremonial was quite modest, and this continued as the practice of the Tractarian leaders.

It was under the influence of John Mason Neale and others associated with the Cambridge Movement that external aspects of the liturgy came to be a major concern. As we have seen, the preoccupations of the Tractarians lay in the affirmation of, for them, critical theological aspects of the place of the Church and sacraments in the Christian life. This concern for the recovery of the authentic sacramental tradition laid the foundation, of course, for the use of external forms of liturgical expression which such a theology seemed to demand. But to a great extent customary Anglican ceremonial had been radically undermined by the rationalism of the Latitudinarians. The renewal brought by the Evangelicals, with its strong emphasis on the internal work of the Spirit and its characteristic suspicion of external ceremonies, permitted the 'high and dry' character of Anglican worship to remain intact.

The theology of the Tractarians, however, and the principles espoused by the leaders of the Cambridge Movement soon created an imperative for external expressions in the liturgy which had long ceased to be familiar to Anglicans. In our discussion of the Cambridge Ecclesiologists, we noted Neale's opinion that the recovery of Gothic architecture in churches would lead to an awareness of 'the poverty of our present vestments'.[27] In most cases, the 'present vestments' of which Neale spoke probably included at best the cassock (or gown), surplice and scarf. The cope had fallen into disuse even at cathedrals from the mid-eighteenth century, as was yet more clearly the case in regard to the chasuble. Certainly the vestments commonly used in the early nineteenth century lacked the richness of design which characterized the style of vesture admired by the ritualists.[28] Neale remained a leader of the ritualist movement, both in regard to liturgical aspects of church design and in the use of the chasuble in the celebration of the Eucharist. Yet it is important to remember that this was no superficial concern for externals on Neale's part. The impact of the Oxford Movement had clearly established the priority of theological issues, as we see in Neale's insistence upon the doctrine of baptismal regeneration and its express foundation in the formularies of the Prayer Book.[29]

When Anglicans wished to incorporate external expressions of the renewed sacramental theology into their liturgical practices, the simple fact was that Rome offered an authoritative resource in these matters. The centuries following the Reformation have been called, by various historians of the Roman rite, 'the age of rubricism'. Perhaps in reaction to the threat to papal authority which the Reformation represented, a medieval tendency to restrict liturgical law to Roman jurisdiction came to full term in the Council of Trent with its revision and promulgation of official liturgical rites and norms as universally binding. The rites became fixed within a complex of canon and rubrical laws which indicated in the most authoritative terms the norms of liturgical practice down to the most minute details. Given the vacuum which characterized Anglican practice in such matters, it is not surprising that Anglicans who sought guidance in regard to externals would turn to this formidable resource. In the Tracts themselves we find a pro-Roman disposition in this regard, as, for example, in a very positive approach to the Roman breviary as a source for Christian devotion and the basis upon which Morning and Evening Prayer in the Church of England were formed. This sympathetic attitude toward the Roman liturgical heritage grew stronger through the activity of various priests who were willing to test the issue to its limits.

During the decade following the 1833 origin of the Oxford Movement, many men trained by the Tractarian leaders went out into the pastoral ministry of the Church of England. This opened the way for a shift of focus for the movement from the academic world at Oxford to the pastoral life of the Church at large. This shift led to an incorporation of many of the concerns of the Cambridge Movement, in regard not merely to architecture but also to the whole range of external factors which came to be seen as the necessary articulations of Tractarian theological views. This involved a greater concern for questions of ritual than had characterized the situation at Oxford, but it was an evolution thoroughly grounded in the sacramental theology which we have considered.

During the earliest years of the Oxford Movement, the evidence which we have for the introduction of unfamiliar externals is concerned with matters which from today's perspective seem remarkably innocent of controversial potential. In 1837, for example, Newman introduced an early celebration of the Eucharist at St Mary's at which he used candles on the altar and followed the custom of mixing water with the wine in the chalice. It gives us an insight into the barrenness of Anglican liturgical practices at the time to learn that Newman thereby provoked a protest for introducing a style 'very much after the Romish manner'. Such practices were, however, only the beginning.

The work of the Cambridge Camden Society played a

significant role in these matters from the time of its founding in 1839. The Society's expressed intention, however, was not to introduce Roman Catholic practices but rather to recover for the Church of England an awareness of its own heritage both in medieval architecture and in seventeenth-century ceremonial customs. They published evidence of rites and usages which had continued in Anglican practice after the Reformation and thus could not be taken as incompatible with the faith of the Church. The new churches built under the influence of the Cambridge principles created a context in which this restored ritualism might flourish.

At first ritual practices were limited either to those authorized by the Prayer Book rubrics or to the customs of seventeenth-century Anglicanism. The seventeenth century offered a clearly Anglican model for ritual matters which were in turn based upon primitive practice. William Palmer's *Origines Liturgicae*, to which we referred earlier, had encouraged an interest in the customs associated with the ancient liturgies, and made a rather over-simplified identification between the rites of the Book of Common Prayer and their primitive counterparts. The generative cause of these ritual practices is found primarily in a concern for the beauty and holiness which were believed to characterize the authentic Anglican liturgical tradition. Unfortunately, the controversies which followed upon the introduction of such liturgical customs made the whole ritual issue a symbol for a certain style of churchmanship. As the issue developed, the rather naive praise of the Prayer Book gave way to a more critical viewpoint and a more sympathetic attitude toward Roman practices.

Disaffection with the Book of Common Prayer had far-reaching implications, since the Prayer Book is the basis of the rule of faith and practice in Anglicanism. Suggestions of its inadequacy implied the appropriateness of looking into the rites and beliefs of other religious traditions. The boundaries for liturgical usage were thus enormously expanded, to include not only the indications found in primitive documents and rites, but also those of the contemporary Roman Church. At first, the turn toward Roman liturgical materials was for a kind of devotional supplement to make up the inadequacies of the Prayer Book. Deepened knowledge of the Roman liturgical system revealed in it resources which could profitably be added to Anglican liturgical practice. For the Tractarians, the Roman system gave clear evidence of the underlying sacramental principle which they taught. To be a Catholic was to take part in this sacramental system, and thus, perhaps inevitably, Catholic-minded Anglicans were impelled toward a more or less thorough adoption or adaptation of the Roman liturgical pattern.

Tractarian emphasis upon the principle of sacramental instrumentality involved its adherents in a religious system in which God employs physical realities, persons and things, as instruments of his grace, as the explicit means by which the mystery of divine grace is communicated to mankind. This emphasis, of course, set the Tractarians and their followers in opposition to both the rationalists and the Evangelicals, and at the same time allied them with the fundamental sacramentalism of the Roman Church, and finally with many aspects of its faith and practice. The integral relation between a doctrinal belief and its liturgical expression was always recognized by the Tractarians. Ritual was thus no trivial matter; it was itself a means by which doctrine was proclaimed; its involvement of the body was a means by which the whole person, and not just the mind, was touched by the instruments of God's grace.

If the adoption of Roman liturgical practices by certain members of the Church of England was the cause of deep suspicion at the time and still raises serious questions about the relation of liturgical norms to a wider range of ecclesial matters, it is nevertheless important to acknowledge that the primary aspects of Tractarian theological and liturgical concerns have contributed to the renewal of sacramental and liturgical theology in our own century in significant ways. Their emphasis upon the sacramental principle and its articulation in the Church's liturgical life implies an end to an artificial separation of theory and practice. Their study of primitive sources expanded the range of knowledge of our common liturgical heritage in the early Church. Most important of all, their emphasis upon the doctrine of the Church laid the foundation for the major developments in our sacramental understanding as reflected in current liturgical renewal.

7 The Church as the People of God

From its inception the Oxford Movement was concerned with the question of the nature of the Church. Their appeal to 'the Primitive Church', with their use of the doctrine of Apostolic Succession as a sure link to the Church's early origins, was a means of affirming the authority of the Church in an ever more secularized world. Their defensive posture served a very important purpose as we view the matter from the closing decades of the twentieth century: it led them to engage the question of the doctrine of the Church in a serious, although often tentative, way.

Questions about the Church are so common today that it is difficult to realize that this concern is a comparatively recent development. The official dialogues between the various Christian traditions which have been such an evident fruit of the ecumenical movement have compelled Christians who have been engaged by these questions to explore all the various aspects of the Church's identity to an unprecedented degree. It is not surprising that a number of writers have suggested that the major theological developments of our time find their common focus in the doctrine of the Church. But the source of these developments may be found in the questions which engaged theologians in the nineteenth century, including the Tractarians.

Prior to the raising of the question of the doctrine of the Church in the last century, there had been little effort among theologians to define it or to identify the fundamental elements which constitute its reality. To a great extent, Christians simply lived in the Church within the framework of its given structures. It was conceived, to the degree that it was discussed at all, primarily in terms of its hierarchical structure. To a great extent, it was essentially the clergy who were identified as 'the Church' even in countries where membership in the Church was normal for the entire society. This popular identification of the Church with the clergy is indicative of a mentality which viewed the Church essentially with respect to cultic activity.

In the nineteenth century, theologians began to recover a sense of the Church conceived in sacramental terms and to identify its life with the baptized community, as we have observed in the thought of Newman. The sources for this approach were found in the writings of the early Fathers, whose teaching made a notable contribution to the rediscovery of the Church as the people of God.

The first stage of this recovery was, as we have observed, to propose an idealized and static model for the Church based upon its characteristics in the high Middle Ages, viewed as the most Christian of all eras in human history. This romanticizing of the medieval Church was not the activity merely of the Tractarians, but was part of the whole cultural fabric at the time. The restoration of the Benedictine life at the monastery of Solesmes in France in 1833 was, on the Continent, an expression of the same attitude.

This first stage served the purpose of developing an active awareness of the elements which make up the Church's life. Under the influence of further theological reflection and the force of other factors in the general life of the Church, the static model began to crumble and a dynamic concept of the Church as an organic, living society began to emerge. We noted earlier that it is especially in the sermons of Newman, as contrasted with the narrower approach of the Tracts, that we find a sacramental concept of the Church emerging, a concept of the Church as an instrument in the hands of God, continuing his work in each successive generation.

The sacramental concept of the Church has developed significantly as a foundation for all sacramental theology in this century. At an international theological level, the publication of the encyclical 'On the Mystical Body of Christ' by Pope Pius XII in 1943 marked a major victory for the sacramental understanding of the Church. In the light of more recent developments, the theology of the encyclical evokes much of the old hierarchical model, but for its time the document was a major turning point and was immediately seen to have great ecumenical significance. It proposes a sacramental model of the Church and makes a clear identification of the Church with the whole body of the baptized. It is this renewed concept of the Church which is the foundation for the revised liturgical books of the various churches, and thus establishes the theological framework for future sacramental and liturgical developments.

THE CHURCH AS SACRAMENT

The Church is itself the primary sacrament of Christ in human history. It is the sign of the union of all believers with God the Father, and at the same time it is the sign of the promise of the ultimate unity of the whole of humanity. Its role in human history is as the instrument of an all-encompassing unity which is believed to be God's purpose for the creation. The Church as sign is an anticipation of that purpose: the unity of the Body of Christ is a dynamic process which seeks to draw all generations into its fellowship. The final fulfilment of that goal is signified in images of the consummation of human history at the end of time.

The exalted vocation spoken of here reveals the awesome purpose to which the whole people of God are invited. It exposes the triviality of many of our images of the Church which have been conditioned by the shattered human situation. The Church is not a club for people interested in religion; it is a society established by God as an instrument of his purpose in human history. In this perspective the Church is, as we have seen in the vocabulary of the Tractarians, 'the extension of the Incarnation'. After the Ascension of Christ, the gift of the Holy Spirit is the origin and first principle of the Church's life. The Church is the domain of the Spirit, the instrument through which the Spirit works to draw all mankind to the Father through the fellowship of Christ's Body.

The Church, the Body of Christ, is the context in which the communication of God's gifts to believers takes place. The Church is itself the primary instrument of that communication; it is an instrument of grace. The specific sacraments, especially Baptism and Eucharist, signify the fundamental shaping of the common life: Baptism brings us into the fellowship of the Body through a sacramental identification with the death and resurrection of Christ; the Eucharist builds up our unity in that fellowship through our common nourishment in the one bread and the one cup. The unity thus effected is a sign of that ultimate unity willed by God for his people.

The corporate nature of the Church reflects the belief that God has formed a people to witness to him in the world. In other words, salvation is not a gift to individuals but to a people. There is a mutuality in our lives, first as God's creatures, and still more marvellously as a renewed people of faith. The corporate nature of the Church points to the coinherence of human life, so that we are in a deeply mysterious way instruments of the salvation of which we are also the beneficiaries. God has summoned an assembly of all who look to him in faith. That assembly is the Church, scattered all over the face of the earth and at the same time united in Christ, who is himself the primary witness and the essential sacrament of God's presence in the world.

DIVERSE MINISTRIES IN THE CHURCH

The recovery of a sacramental understanding of the Church places the question of ministry in a new perspective. The hierarchical model of the Church tended to identify ministry with the cultic responsibilities of the ordained bishops, priests and deacons. We saw in the Tractarian emphasis upon the Apostolic Succession a concept of the Church in which the ordained ministry has an importance which virtually subsumes other aspects of the Church's life. Not only does this isolate the ordained ministries from other forms of ministry in the Church, but it also isolates one aspect of the meaning of apostolicity from the wider dimensions of its meaning. Apostolicity is a gift to the Church for the building up of its life through a special form of service.

The renewed awareness of the identity of the Church as the whole people of God makes Baptism the decisive turning point of Christian faith and commitment. The authentic model for all Christians is Jesus' own life of service. All those baptized into Christ share in his ministry, but the diversity of gifts given by the Holy Spirit to the various members of the Church implies a wide diversity in the forms of ministry. A recent ecumenical document summarizes the matter in these words:

> The Holy Spirit bestows on the community diverse and complementary gifts. These are for the common good of the whole people and are manifested in acts of service within the community and to the world. They may be gifts of communicating the Gospel in word and deed, gifts of healing, gifts of praying, gifts of teaching and learning, gifts of serving, gifts of guiding and following, gifts of inspiration and vision. All members are called to discover with the help of the community, the gifts they have received and to use them for the service of the world to which the Church is sent.[30]

The static view of Apostolic Succession which we found in Tractarian teaching fell into the trap of implying that it is a valid ministry which establishes a valid church. But in the renewed ecclesiology which we see reflected in the above quotation, it is the Holy Spirit who is the source of validity (if such a concept is even appropriate), and certainly it is the Holy Spirit who is the source of the gifts of ministry which build up the Body.

The relation of diverse ministries to the life of the Church is one of the primary areas in which current reflection demonstrates a dramatic shift from the narrow preoccupations fostered by the static model. The recovery of a sense of the necessity and complementarity of diverse ministries is one of the major signs of an enlarged view of the Church's life in which all members are instruments of God's action in the world. There is an enormous task of education to be done if all the baptized are to be brought to the realization that they only are the Church. For many centuries the word has referred to a sacred building or to a hierarchy of ordained officials who have conceived the Church's life primarily in terms of their cultic ministries as the suppliers of sacred commodities to otherwise passive laity. The use of the word 'church' with either of those meanings dominating is an indication of the terrible loss of the sense of the meaning of the word in the New Testament.

To be the Church is to share a common life sustained by a common faith, not as isolated individuals, but as a people who share a participation in the death and resurrection of Jesus, who share the celebration of his Gospel, who share the problems and joys which are part of every human life, and finally who share a common mission, a common ministry as agents of transformation in the world.

Such a model cannot come into being as a theory, but only within the varied realities which shape each local church. Members of the Church who perceive the importance of a recovery of this New Testament model must take on the task of implementing its norms whenever and wherever possible. Only through such a groundswell of commitment can the Church recover the signs of its true nature.

8 The Meaning of Baptism

There is probably no area of liturgical renewal of more far-reaching importance than that which is taking place in the theology and practice of Christian initiation. We saw that for the Tractarians, the primary issue was their general concern that Baptism and the other sacraments are truly instruments of grace, not merely supplementary religious rituals. Their concern was centred on the issue of sacramental meaning, that the sacramental rites truly effect what they signify. In regard to Baptism, the key issue which was the test of meaning was that of baptismal regeneration.

Theological reflection upon Baptism in recent years has expanded the range of issues which are entwined in this subject, but certainly Baptism has emerged dramatically as a critical turning point in the life of a Christian, and not merely a brief and often private act of dedication. The most important aspect of the issue has been the recovery of a sense of the relation of an individual's Baptism to the corporate life of the Church, an aspect of its meaning which we shall explore here.

At the most basic level, Baptism is an incorporation into Christ which is at the same time an incorporation into his Body, the Church. It unites the person baptized with Christ and with his people. As participation in the risen life of Jesus, Baptism is a sign of a new birth, of the washing away of sin, of enlightenment, and of the outpouring of the Holy Spirit. It is a sign of freedom from bondage and an entrance into a new humanity where divisions according to race, sex or social rank are abolished. All such images are reflective of a wonderfully rich sign of the varied means of God's purpose.

To speak of Baptism as a participation in the death and resurrection of Jesus is to speak of the profound identification which exists between Christ and each member of his Body. The image of a passage through death evokes the Old Testament origins of the doctrine of Baptism in the exodus experience of the Jewish people as God's act of liberation. The image of death also suggests the sign of Baptism as a forgiveness of sin, a moral washing by which a person receives the gifts of pardon, cleansing and sanctification. The link between death and the forgiveness of sin is seen in Baptism as the effective sign of death to a self-centred life, the purification of that sinful self and a rebirth to a life centred in God and offered in service to others. The gift of sanctification refers to the work of the Holy Spirit in the lives of believers. That work of the Spirit is not limited to a liturgical moment, but precedes and follows the rite as well as being articulated sacramentally in the initiatory rite. The Spirit sustains the baptized person in the life of faith, so it is through the Spirit that we live out our Baptism. The living out of one's Baptism takes place within the bond of unity as one people who witness to and serve the one Lord in all parts of the world.

BAPTISM AND FAITH

The relation of Baptism to faith was a source of dispute between the Tractarians and the Evangelicals. Because of their concern for the instrumentality of the sacraments, the Tractarians affirmed the most intimate relation between inner faith and the external rite. As we saw in Newman's *Lectures on Justification*, faith is the internal instrument of the justification for which Baptism is the external instrument. For the Evangelicals, such a view suggested a rejection of the doctrine of justification by faith alone.

An emerging ecumenical consensus in recent decades has placed this question within a larger context. All the churches affirm that faith is a necessity for the salvation which is embodied in the rites of Christian initiation. Mature membership in the Body of Christ requires a true personal commitment. The rite of Baptism must not be isolated from the implications of such mature participation in the Church's life. It is not a brief ritual experience, but rather an ongoing growth into Christ. The work of the Holy Spirit is not focused in a magic moment but is rather the gradual and progressive work of transformation. The life of a Christian involves a continuing engagement with the experience of God's grace and the demands imposed by the response of faith. Maturing in faith is a lifelong process of which it is quite appropriate to speak as an entrance into the meaning of one's Baptism.

Such a maturing in faith is a sign that human beings can be regenerated, born anew, not in an isolated moment of conversion, although some persons do experience dramatic turning points in their lives, but in an organic, lived process of growth in Christ. Out of that experience of renewal and also of liberation which they perceive in themselves, mature Christians are impelled to bear witness to Christ on the basis not of a dry intellectualism but of an immediate personal experience. This witness takes place within the Church for mutual nurture in faith, but also flows out from that common life as witness to the world and service in the world.

The full significance of our Baptism cannot be grasped in a moment. It is explored as we live out the implications of faith as members of the Christian family. These implications are not narrowly religious in their content. They are not fulfilled through a multiplicity of religious or cultic activities, although the authentic liturgical act has a wonderful power to remind us of the wider meaning of our commitment of faith. We come to see that Baptism has serious ethical implications which involve us in the fostering of God's will in all the dimensions of human life.

To see Baptism in such a comprehensive framework frees us from too limited a preoccupation with a primary internal faith-moment or external ritual moment, for the internal and external aspects come to be seen as deeply complementary and integrated in meaning. Neither should be isolated from an awareness that both the gift of faith and its sacramental signification in the baptismal rite are ordered toward a lifelong commitment, to an ever-deepening grasp of the meaning of faith and its sacramental signification in a transformed life.

THE QUESTION OF INFANT BAPTISM

The understanding of Baptism proposed above also places the question of infant Baptism within a broader framework. Once it is accepted that Baptism is the engagement of a person to a lifelong process of spiritual growth within the community of faith, then we recognize that at the time of Baptism all of us are 'as newborn babes', whatever our age may happen to be. Although an adult is able to make a confession of faith, that does not indicate that the person has already reached a mature awareness of the full meaning of the confession. It is, as we have seen, in the life context that the confession will be polished and refined as it is nurtured and tested within the corporate life of the Church.

In the case of the Baptism of an infant, the rite emphasizes God's initiative, which is the generative source of the rite, and the corporate faith of the whole body of believers. Further, in a significant way, the faith which the child is heir to through the faith of its parents is exemplified. Theologians speak of infant Baptism as 'proleptic', that is, as an act which anticipates its completion in the personal confession of faith which will be made when the child comes to maturity. In the case of infants, the period of formation which would normally precede the Baptism of adults becomes a pastoral imperative to be fulfilled at an appropriate age after Baptism.

In both instances, the Baptism of an adult or an infant, the person will be expected to grow in the understanding of faith under the pastoral guidance of the Church's ministry. For the adult as much as for the infant, the rite of Baptism does not mark an end to a completed act, but implies the necessity of continuing growth in the personal response of faith which always involves the relation of the individual to the Christian community. Growth in personal faith and a committed participation in the life of the Church are essential if Baptism is to bear the fruit which its meaning promises.

The importance of growth in understanding of the faith spoken of above reminds us of what is probably the most critical failure in the history of baptismal practice, the loss of the period of formation (known as the catechumenate) during the time when adults were the usual candidates for Baptism. Baptism was the ritual climax to a full preparatory ministry, often of three years' duration, during which the foundations for incorporation into the Church were laid down. There was no imperative to rush to the font because the attachment of Baptism to a fear of death and the forgiveness of what was known as original sin had not yet taken hold of the Church's intepretation of Baptism. The rite was understood into the fifth century as being an act which established a relation to the whole body, and thus involved a rather extensive preparation, a type of Christian socialization, for that anticipated incorporation.

The gradual emergence of infant Baptism as the more familiar pattern of initiation in an increasingly Christianized society dealt a death blow to the ecclesial shaping which was accomplished through the catechumenate. With most people already baptized as infants, the formative ministry which was to culminate in a public profession of faith was at first trivialized by being reduced to a few vestigial liturgical elements and finally lost entirely. At the time of the Reformation, many of the reformers were deeply troubled by the lack of basic Christian knowledge among the great majority of the laity. The development of the various catechisms was an attempt to confront the problem and to establish at least some minimal standards for Christian formation. Unfortunately, the general cultural situation and the then current approach to theology led to a minimal expectation, and a question-and-answer approach to fundamental matters of faith which require a more nuanced understanding. The further matter which the classical catechumenate addressed, the transformation of life-style which was implied by faith in Christ, was to a great extent lost and was replaced by a rigid moralism.

There is probably no greater imperative before the Church today than the revival of a ministry equal to the ancient catechumenate in intent. Contemporary society cannot adopt the same models as those which were effective in the third or fourth centuries, but the meaning of Baptism which has been proposed here can never be implemented if the rite continues to be normally isolated from the wider framework of ministry represented by the catechumenate.

The purposes of a restored catechumenate may be briefly summarized. First, it is a time of evangelization during which the imperatives of the Gospel are set before the 'catechumens', that is, those who are undergoing the process of pre-baptismal formation. Although the title 'catechumen' is not appropriate for one who is already baptized, it is even more inappropriate to think that the practice of infant Baptism eliminates the need, albeit at a later time, for the type of formation which an authentic catechumenate offers.

The catechumenate is concerned with the communication of the Church's faith, the fundamentals of Christian life and teaching, not merely a set of facts about the Church. This suggests that there must be a preparation for the catechumenate, a time in which the intention to share in the faith of the Church is clarified and given some coherent articulation. From the very start, a high level of pastoral discernment must be exercised. People should not be pushed to move along quickly or automatically, as is sometimes the case with a class in school. What is involved is the ground-laying for the person's whole future life as a Christian. It is the foundation upon which the Christian life will be lived.

The central purpose of the catechumenate is the communication to the next generation of Christians of the paschal mystery, the central affirmation at the heart of Christian faith and practice. The living Lord is the content of the mystery, the Lord who was incarnate in human history and who now continues to proclaim and teach, to baptize and offer thanksgiving through the instrument of his Church. A restored catechumenate is an imperative for the recovery of a truly ecclesial sacramental theology because it preserves Christian practice from too narrow an identification with cultic acts, and affirms the intimate connections between the faith of the Church and all aspects of human life. A vigorous catechumenate is a safeguard against a superficial model of the Church, and enables the sacramental signs to be celebrated with regard to the full range of their meaning.

9 Confirmation

In a brief work of this kind, it would be impossible to discuss in detail the understanding of the sacraments presented here to all the sacramental acts of the Church. Our attention throughout the book rests upon Baptism and the Eucharist, which have a primacy in Anglicanism as being 'ordained of Christ our Lord in the Gospel' (Article XXV). Other rites 'commonly called Sacraments' include Confirmation, Penance, Holy Orders, Matrimony and Unction. Because of its particular role in Anglican pastoral ministry, and because its history raises questions with regard to both Baptism and Eucharist, it is important for us to consider how Confirmation fits in with the approach to sacramental practice which is presented here.

First, given the focus of this book upon the teaching of the Oxford Movement, it is interesting to note the minor role taken by Confirmation among the subjects discussed in the Tracts for the Times. The only concentrated material is found in Tract 42, which is a reprinting of 'Bishop [Thomas] Wilson's Meditations on his Sacred Office'. Wilson (1633–1755) saw Confirmation as 'the perfection of baptism', and the occasion on which the Holy Spirit is conveyed by the imposition of hands to 'such as are rightly prepared to receive such a blessing, as at the first He came visibly upon those that had been baptized'. Wilson thus sees the activity of the Holy Spirit in Confirmation as complementary to the work of the Spirit in Baptism, Confirmation somehow completing or perfecting Baptism. The meaning of this completion is not made clear except that it is 'to shed further influences on those that receive it, for stirring up the gift of God bestowed in baptism'. The only other

75

significant assertions made by Bishop Wilson, and supported by the Tractarians in their republication of his 'Meditations', is that Confirmation was instituted by Christ in continuation of the Jewish *bar mitzvah* at the age of thirteen. Wilson sees the practice of Confirmation attested in the book of Acts, and as necessary as Baptism 'even in the Apostles' times'.

Although we see a firm pastoral diligence in Bishop Wilson's teaching on Confirmation, we also see some rather naive presuppositions about the biblical material to which he refers, and a consequent misunderstanding of the origins of the practice. Our knowledge in these areas has greatly expanded during the last several decades, especially under the impact of the discovery of early documents which fully depict the structure of the process of Christian initiation. Confirmation, as the medieval Church came to know it, and as it was in turn modified within the Anglican tradition, is now seen as a constantly evolving practice which reflected the Church's adaptation to changed situations. In fact we find, as the American theologian Urban Holmes has characterized it, that Confirmation is 'a rite in search of a reason'. The early liturgical pattern for Christian initiation involved a customary three-year catechumenate which offered a time for the radical re-orientation of life-style on the part of the catechumens before they became candidates for Baptism during the six weeks prior to Easter, at which time they were to be baptized. The culminating rite during the Easter vigil was a multi-faceted liturgical celebration which brought the process of Christian formation to a climax. In addition to numerous complementary elements, there were three primary ritual expressions in the Baptism: the water rite, the laying on of hands by the bishop, and the reception of the Eucharist. These three elements *together* formed the integral sacramental celebration. All available evidence indicates that a separate laying on of hands by a bishop at another time was unknown until several centuries later.

When a distinct rite of Confirmation appeared, its separation from the water rite was brought about primarily through practical realities in a now much larger Church in which the bishop could not be present at all celebrations of Christian initiation. Once separated, however, the rite of Confirmation began to develop a theology of its own, and the Church lost a sense of the origin of the bishop's laying on of hands in the baptismal rite itself. Confirmation came to have a distinct identity, but was constantly a cause of concern to conscientious bishops during the medieval period because it seldom enjoyed popular support among the laity. In the common medieval religious attitude, Confirmation was often seen as a kind of optional rite, somehow related to Baptism, yet not really an obligation.

The bishops enacted various types of legislation to enforce the Church's expectation that Confirmation would be administered to each member of the Church at an appropriate age. One such bishop was John Peckham (c. 1225–92), Archbishop of Canterbury, who directed that baptized Christians might not receive Communion until they were confirmed by a bishop. This regulation was without precedent, and was merely an attempt to enforce conformity to the Church's discipline. The regulation was taken into the Prayer Book tradition by Thomas Cranmer, Peckham's successor some three centuries later in the See of Canterbury, in the words: 'And there shall be none admitted to the Holy Communion, until such time as he be confirmed, or be ready and desirous to be confirmed'.

Cranmer, however, had not left the medieval rite of Confirmation intact. Recent study of his work suggests that the archbishop took a bold step to restore the laying on of hands to its relationship with the water rite. He inserted a signing of the candidate with a cross on the forehead immediately after the water rite, accompanied by a form which was closely modelled on the late medieval theology of Confirmation, especially in its reference to the newly baptized as 'Christ's faithful soldier and servant' who was 'to confess the faith of Christ crucified, and manfully to fight under his banner against sin, the world, and the devil". Cranmer presumed that the parish priest would be the normal minister of Baptism, but he gave the Church of England a rite which was clearly a complete rite of Christian initiation. The idea that newly baptized infants should also receive Communion as part of their Baptism did not present itself because the practice had fallen into disuse for several centuries, and also because of the Reformers' concern for the development of an adequate level of understanding prior to the first reception of the Eucharist.

Yet in addition to this shift of the sense of medieval Confirmation back into the water rite, Cranmer also kept a rite of Confirmation in the Prayer Book. The Anglican Church espoused the teaching that only Baptism and Eucharist are sacraments in the full sense, that is, ordained by Christ. Cranmer did not believe Confirmation to be a sacrament, but out of what was perhaps a strong political sense decided to include a rite by that title which had been fostered so firmly by his predecessors. This may be the source of a certain ambiguity which has always existed in Anglican Confirmation and which has permitted a variety of interpretations. Cranmer retained the bishop as minister of the new Confirmation rite, with the prayer for the sevenfold gifts of the Spirit and the laying on of hands. Nevertheless, an examination of his rite reveals it to bear only an obscure relation to medieval Confirmation, and to be far more clearly a rite which marks the time when children, baptized in infancy, have reached an age of a certain rational understanding of basic aspects of Christian faith, and who can recite the Lord's Prayer, the Apostles' Creed, and the Ten Commandments. What we have, in effect, is a reaffirmation of one's baptismal commitment at the end of a process of basic Christian formation. In this perspective, we see Anglican Confirmation to be quite complementary in purpose to the concern of the Reformers in general that all Christians receive some basic catechetical formation and profess a commitment to Christ as an indication of their taking upon themselves their baptismal covenant. It is a rite of maturity.

Given this de-emphasis upon any sacramental under-standing of Confirmation by Anglicans generally, it is not surprising that it was often overlooked in practice or else performed in very perfunctory ways. From the period of the Restoration onward in England, theological writers virtually ignored the rite. The pastoral concern for Con-firmation which we observed in the writings of Bishop Thomas Wilson is limited to a small number of bishops who were affected by the old high church tradition. From there it fed directly into the concerns of the Oxford Move-ment, as a practice to be observed because of its presumed apostolic origin. It is only in recent years that the fruit of our increased knowledge of the rites of initiation has led to further theological reflection and ultimately to the reform of the rites in the light of that knowledge.

It is obvious that our pattern for the process of Christian initiation today cannot simply duplicate the pattern of the early centuries, but our knowledge of that pattern raises serious questions which require attention and which should be allowed to illuminate our understanding of the making of a Christian. First, we see that a rite cannot be removed from the wider context of Christian formation and life-style. In other words, the ministry accomplished in the first centuries through the catechumenate is an impera-tive for today, even if our cultural situation requires appropriate adaptations. The ritual does not stand alone, but rather marks the fulfilment of a responsible ministry of Christian formation.

Second, the early pattern of initiation reveals the essential and underlying unity of all sacramental rites as signs of the sacramental nature of the Church itself. A splintered sacramental theology which gazes too closely at one sacramental act loses a sense of this interconnected-ness. For the first several centuries, baptismal candidates experienced an extended and rich succession of rites which articulated a process of formation and culminated in a rite of initiation which proclaimed above all else the nature of the Church into which the candidates were being in-corporated. Our pattern today, in spite of adaptations to particular conditions, must clearly express the Church's identity as a communion of faith. The process of formation and the rites of initiation must develop out of a deep sense of the corporate nature of the Body of Christ.

THE ROLE OF CHILDREN IN WORSHIP

The catechumenate is concerned with a ministry of Christian maturity. Its purpose is to establish a context in which those who are to be baptized may come to an adequate sense of the confession of faith which they are about to make. The Baptism of infants, which we spoke of as proleptic, or anticipatory, raises a complementary set of questions. Often children have been treated as essentially passive Christians until they have reached a certain age at which they are accepted as appropriate subjects in sacramental acts. This implies a separation between Baptism and all other sacramental acts which is impossible to justify in terms of the renewed theology of the sacraments which has been presented.

If the worship of the Church is the prayer-action of all its baptized members, children are not a nuisance; they are a necessary part of this varied human family. And if they are a necessary part, then it is not so that they may be locked into the rigidities of worship as it is generally conceived. Children must be permitted to bring their own unique gifts into the Christian family's celebration of God's presence in Christ and the Spirit.

This is not an isolated problem about how to introduce children to full participation in the liturgy. What is involved is a fundamental issue of Christian self-understanding: what does it mean to be the Church? Children, by their human nature and Baptism, are appropriate liturgical participants even in infancy. If they are not, then it is virtually impossible to justify the Church's unbroken tradition of infant Baptism. In fact, that tradition pleads for full participation by all members of the Body. All the known evidence suggests that the practice of infant Baptism grew out of the strong significance of the family unit in early Christian society and led immediately to full sacramental membership.

In more recent practice, children have been treated as pre-liturgical persons. Although we baptize infants, their full participation in the Eucharist (that is, the reception of the sacrament) is delayed until some rational response is forthcoming. We make this rational response an essential prerequisite for full sacramental participation in the Christian life. In so emphasizing this aspect of human response, we obscure the important roles played by other dimensions of the whole person, including the affective and intuitive powers which children manifest at an early age. In this regard, children are not the only victims. The emphasis upon the primacy of a rational response is integral to the liturgical mentality which has dominated the Church's prayer for several centuries.

The inclusion of children as integral participants in parish liturgy may work for the salvation of the adults and certainly for their wholeness as worshippers. For centuries a false liturgical mentality has permitted us to forget that we have bodies, that we are physical persons, and that our worship involves us with each other and not merely in perfectly ordered, cerebral ways. We need to learn and live the meaning of Tertullian's phrase, 'the flesh is the hinge of salvation'. Children bring a naturalness to the liturgy which judges our overformalized routines. Until they are pressed into behavioral moulds, they bring a wonderful openness to the experience of word and gesture, touch and movement — to the whole array of human elements which lie at the heart of the liturgical act. Their feelings find articulation in the corporate context, since they have not learned to put on a religious mask.

From the human side, this whole range of participation rests only in minimal ways upon words and rational understanding. Are we therefore to say that a child's participation is meaningless? Is a person not capable of receiving God's gifts until rational understanding is reached? If so, why do we baptize infants? Have we in our pastoral norms lost touch with what the tradition of infant baptism means? Is not the newborn child really a member of the human family? If so, can we not see that the newly baptized child is really a member of the Christian family?

Our consistent liturgical practice in the Baptism of infants challenges us to live its implications at the practical/pastoral level, with all the difficulties that may involve. We must begin by recognizing the anomaly of our custom of baptizing infants and immediately denying them the Eucharist. Having Baptism take place at a Family Eucharist at which the newly baptized do not receive the sacrament only intensifies the anomaly. Surely the absurdity of this juxtaposition must soon lead us to see that the justification of infant baptism rests upon the same premises as those which justify infant communion.

Yet the participation of children in the liturgy is not merely a question of their reception of the Eucharist. Nor is that participation of concern only to parents, as though it were merely the religious dimension of family life. The importance of the participation of children reaches to a still deeper level. Christian worship concerns the whole Christian family, the full membership of the Church. Although the presence of children worshipping with their parents is important, that presence is also important for single persons, for the elderly, and for all who make up the parish community. Children have an integral place in worship which bears significance for the corporate prayer of the whole Church. When that significance is understood, it will require a revolution in our patterns of Sunday worship.

Liturgy as the faith-actions of the Christian community is not a drill delegated to clerical specialists, but is rather the meeting point of the whole community both to celebrate its faith and at the same time to have that faith nourished by word and sacrament. In this light, the experience of liturgy becomes far more significant than merely verbal explanations about the liturgy. Children should not be excluded because they do not yet understand. Let them experience the liturgy from infancy; understanding will come later.

82

Interestingly enough, this is precisely the pattern which the first several centuries of the Church followed with both adults and children. The mystery of God's action in Baptism and Eucharist was first experienced, and only then was explanation given. The catechumenate was not concerned with instruction in the sacraments, but rather with the reordering of one's life toward Christ as centre, often involving the putting aside of any occupation which was incompatible with a Christian life-style. Instruction on the sacraments was given only after the neophyte had experienced them. For centuries we have turned this order around in our pattern of Christian formation, and the results are disastrous. Liturgy has ceased to be the natural activity of the Christian, but rather a quite peculiar set of religious customs performed on Sundays. Our contemporary situation requires the common sense which we see at work in the pattern of the early centuries. The candidates passed through a long period of socialization during which an organic process of the assimilation of Christian values might take place. The liturgy, when at last it was experienced, was the ritual expression of that whole organic development. The impact of the signs was not merely in their dramatic enactment but more radically in their articulation of the experience of conversion.

When liturgy is apprehended first through experience, the appropriateness of the full participation of children is evident. Children experience much that they cannot verbally articulate. We do not delay the first bath until the child understands hygiene, nor do we require knowledge of nutrition prior to the first meal. The child experiences many baths and many meals — really experiences them — and at the most basic human level apprehends their meaning through the experience.

Similarly, children experience in the liturgy human actions into which they enter in day-to-day life as members of a family: greeting, embracing, gathering with the family, listening to a good story, asking forgiveness, saying thank-you, washing, eating, celebrating. Yet how often these direct parallels between daily life and Christian worship are suffocated by our prepackaged approach to liturgy. The liturgical experience of children is formative. If the underlying human gestures of the liturgy are minimalized through excessive formalization, the child will experience the Christian faith as alien to human life, a separate religious category which is not directly related to the fabric of day-to-day living.

Attitudes towards family, the table, and sharing a meal are learned through constant experience in the home. If the eating of a meal is normally a private matter for meeting a physical need, or if the gathering of the family is not experienced as a joyful expression of a common life, how can we ever expect the obvious parallels with the Sunday Eucharist to be realized and bear fruit? The best family liturgy on Sunday morning cannot alone convey to children the meaning of Christian life and prayer. It should be learned at home. If we once know the simple joy of sharing in the prayer of a family that prays as part of its daily life, we experience the depth of its importance. As long as prayer is absent or artificialized in the home, there is little hope that Sunday worship can be other than a religious routine of no real meaning in life.

The full incorporation of children into our corporate prayer will require an enormous change of mentality on the part of the Church at large. It will elicit a deeper sensitivity to the non-verbal dimensions of worship. It will require an end to stuffy formality. Best of all, it will help us to discover the naturalness of Christian liturgical prayer and its integral relation to all that is most fully human in our lives.

10 The Eucharist

The deepened awareness of the relation of sacraments to the life of the Church which has emerged in contemporary theology has, inevitably, led to a placing of questions concerning the Eucharist into a different framework from that which was operative at the time of the Tractarians.

The question of the presence of Christ in the Eucharist, for example, has ceased to isolate discussion around the issue merely of the meaning of that presence in regard to the consecrated gifts of bread and wine. Theologians have placed the question of the sacramental presence in the wider context of the modes in which the presence of Christ is manifested within the life of the Church. This moves the whole subject away from a too narrow limitation to the nature of the objectivity of the presence in the bread and wine into a more comprehensive view which sees the sacramental gifts as the focus of a total act of thanksgiving offered by the gathered Church. Similarly the role of the priest as the proclaimer of the eucharistic prayer is no longer isolated from the active participation of all the faithful in what is essentially a corporate action.

The Eucharist as the focus of an intense private piety has, under the impact of a renewed theology of the Church, given way to an affirmation of the Eucharist as primarily an action rather than a sacred object. The title 'Eucharist' refers first of all to the action of the faithful who have gathered: the offering of thanksgiving to the Father as the source of all good. The bread and wine are the focus of that thanksgiving through the role played in the Church's corporate memory by the Last Supper. The gifts of bread and wine support an awesome range of associations from the whole of the Church's life, but the gifts must not be isolated from the fuller dimensions of thanksgiving.

When St Augustine said, 'You are the bread on the altar', he spoke from an insight whose importance we have only recently begun to recover. The first *place* of the Lord's presence is in his people: 'Where two or three are gathered together, there am I in the midst of them.' The presence of Christ in the eucharistic gifts must be linked to this affirmation of his presence among his people. We do not gather to *make* Jesus sacramentally present. Rather, in our gathering as the people of God he is himself present through his identification with us.

Christ is thus present in his Church through a variety of modes. Through the instrumentality of his members, it is Christ who preaches and teaches, it is Christ who ministers and heals, it is Christ who baptizes and who offers himself as our spiritual food. To speak in this way is to see Christ's presence manifested through all the aspects of the Church's life, building up its unity and sending it forth in service to the world.

The much-debated question of the sacrificial nature of the Eucharist is clarified by this concept of presence. The death and resurrection are a once-and-for-all event in human history; his oblation was the one perfect sacrifice offered for the redemption of the world. There is no question of a repetition of that sacrifice, but there is the question of how it is brought to bear upon the faith-experience of each generation of the Church.

As physical and thus sacramental beings, persons for whom material things may support an intensity of meaning, the total action of the Eucharist permits a community of Christians to share in a tangible way with his sacrifice. Just as in Baptism each one of us becomes 'another Christ', so in the common celebration of the Eucharist those who are united in him share in the gracious union with God given to us through Christ's sacrifice. In that common celebration, the Church *remembers* the whole work of God in Christ in a very dynamic sense: through physical/experiential means we are revealed as Christ's body on earth, joined in a common faith and the proclamation of a common thanksgiving.

In this perspective, the eucharistic prayer plays a role of primary significance. It is not merely a formula of consecration to effect a narrowly objective presence of Christ in the eucharistic gifts. Rather, it is a proclamation of faith bearing an importance which is parallel to the proclamation of scripture. The eucharistic prayer is a summary of the basic beliefs which bring the individuals into the common eucharistic action. The transforming power of the Holy Spirit which the prayer proclaims is witness to the Spirit's same transforming power in the lives of the faithful.

The Eucharist is both a fulfilment and a promise: a fulfilment of our Lord's assurance that he will be with his Church to the end of the ages, and the promise of a coming and final consummation in the heavenly banquet of which the Eucharist is a foretaste. From first to last, it is the act of the whole Church, head and members, and the source of nourishment for God's pilgrim people.

Such an approach to the Eucharist suggests a reassessment of certain practices which have been, among Catholic Churchmen, expressions of a strong eucharistic piety, as, for example, Benediction of the Blessed Sacrament or devotions before the Reserved Sacrament. To understand the Eucharist primarily as the action of the Church obliges us to deal with the objective sacredness of the consecrated bread and wine, and the appropriateness of acts of devotion directed toward them. At the heart of the eucharistic action, the Church centres its great thanksgiving on simple gifts of food and drink, signs of human nourishment which have been taken and transformed by the power of God as signs of his abiding presence among his people. The discernment of the divine presence presumes an active faith in the people who gather to offer thanks to God for his work in creation and redemption through Christ. The Church's self-offering is their fundamental act of praise in union with Christ, but in that offering the gifts of bread and wine carry a dazzling specificity. They must not, of course, be narrowly objectified; their full significance always lies in their relation to the Church's faith and self-offering.

If a vigorous sacramental sense has been shaped through appropriate catechesis, then such practices as Benediction can be seen as a kind of overflowing from the central act of thanksgiving. The important place taken by the Eucharist in the Church's life pleads for a rather wide range of expressions of its centrality. As we recover a sense of the Eucharist as the great sign of the unity of God's people, we find that in its awesome simplicity — the sharing of broken bread and a common cup — it is a meeting place for persons of widely different temperaments and spiritual needs, and that the forms of piety which it engenders may vary greatly. What is crucial for all is the common affirmation which unites us in Christ, that this is the bread of life and the cup of salvation.

11 Liturgy and its Social Dimensions

The connections between the liturgy and the service of the under-privileged, the dispossessed, or those suffering from any form of human need have always been there. If the Incarnation is the assertion that God has entered into the context of human history for the work of salvation, then Christians who are united to that work through Baptism are also committed to the service of mankind. If the Eucharist is the act in which Christians celebrate a shared identity in Christ, who came to serve, then our participation in the common life of the Church suggests a self-giving for the good of others, a reaching out to draw others into the Christian fellowship. Service and mission are thus two necessary indications of a commitment of faith which takes the form of more than words.

If these connections are, in fact, rather clear, and have been taught and preached countless times, why has there existed such a chasm between the liturgical profession of faith of which Christian worship is a sign, and the profession of faith in the action of service to those in need? The chasm has existed, at least in part, because of the individualized piety which we have discussed. A narrowly vertical piety which concerns only God and the believer permits an indifference to those around me, be they the rest of the faithful who have gathered at the liturgy with me, or those perhaps more distant persons who are destitute or in grave human need. There are, of course, generous persons who reach out to those in need, but the point is that Christian faith demands articulation in the service of others just as much as it finds expression in ritual forms. The integrity of each rests upon their essential mutuality.

Without such personal involvement in service, membership in the Church becomes narrowly defined by participation in ritual acts. There is a split between profession and action which, in the end, gives the lie to authentic faith.

Early in this century, Bishop Frank Weston of Zanzibar spoke of the importance of a commitment to Christ extending beyond that expressed in liturgical services, 'over the whole area of our life'. He spoke of a self-centredness which is often allied to a highly developed individualized piety, and called for its transformation through commitment to problems of injustice, inequity, or need, and to the building up of true fellowship. Bishop Weston spoke of a kind of moral split in persons who can perform acts of devotion, but who cheat in daily life or are indifferent to the victims of social evils. Finally, in words which still ring with passionate conviction, he said,

> If you are prepared to fight for the right of adoring Jesus in his Blessed Sacrament, then you have got to come out from before your Tabernacle and walk, with Christ mystically present in you, out into the streets of this country, and find the same Jesus in the people of your cities and your villages. You cannot claim to worship Jesus in the Tabernacle, if you do not pity Jesus in the slum. . . . And it is folly — it is madness — to suppose that you can worship Jesus in the Sacraments and Jesus on the throne of glory, when you are sweating him in the souls and bodies of his children. It cannot be done. . . . Go out and look for Jesus in the ragged, in the naked, in the oppressed and sweated, and in those who have lost hope, in those who are struggling to make good. Look for Jesus. And when you see him, gird yourselves with his towel and try to wash their feet.[31]

Yet such a view was already present in the teaching of the Oxford Movement several decades earlier. In a sermon entitled 'God With Us', E. B. Pusey proclaimed the connection between sacramental worship and the service of the poor in these words:

If we would see Him in His Sacraments, we must see Him also, wherever He has declared Himself to be, and especially in His poor. In them also He is 'with us' still. And so our Church has united mercy to His poor with the Sacrament of His Body and Blood, and bade us, ere we approach to receive Him, to remember Him in His poor, and so, 'loving much', we, who are otherwise unworthy, may be 'much forgiven', we, 'considering' Him in His 'poor and needy', may be permitted to behold Him; and for Him parting with our earthly substance, may be partakers of His Heavenly. Real love to Christ must issue in love to all who are Christ's, and real love to Christ's poor must issue in self-denying acts of love towards them. Casual alms-giving is not Christian charity. Rather, seeing Christ in the poor, the sick, the hungry, the thirsty, the naked, we must, if we can, by ourselves, if not, by others, seek them out, as we would seek Christ, looking for a blessing from it, far greater than any they can gain from our alms. It was promised of old time, as a blessing, 'the poor shall never cease out of the land', and now we know the mercy of this mysterious blessing, for they are the Presence of our Lord.[32]

Although such a perspective is firmly rooted in the first years of the Oxford Movement, and has been taught and preached countless times since, the separation today between piety and action seems as great as ever, and is one of the most urgent problems which a renewed liturgical theology must address. The Church has been victim on a large scale of an inherited and defective liturgical mentality, and its effect has been all the more insidious because it has operated at an unconscious level.

THE AUTHENTIC LITURGICAL ACT

We have given a good deal of attention to the common liturgical attitudes held by Christians in the nineteenth century. To carry the matter a bit further, it is not unjust to suggest that the Church had generally lost a true liturgical sense. Religious practice was understood, as we have seen, as an individual, inward matter which, for those so inclined, had external expression in the official, authorized public liturgy, that is, according to the rites of the official books. In this view, however, the true meaning of liturgy is lost. It is easy to find evidence among nineteenth-century writers that the liturgy was viewed as a private act surrounded by public cermonial, the coinciding of private acts of piety by the number of people gathered. One may see the early sources of this attitude in the unbalanced clericalism of the high Middle Ages, that is, from the twelfth century onwards. This clerical domination of the liturgy crowned a gradually developed passivity among the laity with their total exclusion from any active participation. This clerical domination, ironically, was not really addressed effectively at the Reformation, and an individualistic piety continued in various forms. By the nineteenth century ceremonial, rites and other external matters were viewed as secondary to the private prayer of the individuals gathered. Not surprisingly, the especially pious even saw the ritual as a negative factor, a distraction from true prayer.

The authentic liturgical act turns that piety upside down because it presumes as a starting point the full involvement of all God's people, adults and children, who make up the local church. The presence of other persons — their impinging upon me — is not a distraction in the liturgical act; it is integral, essential to the liturgical act, because it is the corporate prayer-action of all united in what is essentially a single self-offering of the Church. Private prayer is intensely important as a complement to that corporate act, but the two are not the same thing and should not coincide. This calls for a revolution in the attitudes dominant in many of our parishes.

The question which will lead us inevitably to the social implications of the liturgy is: what is the meaning of the religious act which underlies the rite? In other words, what is the foundation from which future imperatives for liturgical renewal will be derived? We may summarize certain fundamental matters as a starting point.

1 The liturgy is the action of a gathered social entity, a body of people.
2 The liturgy involves the whole person of those people gathered: it is not just an activity of the mind, of words and ideas, but must involve the body and its senses.
3 The liturgy is ritual prayer: time, place, objects, gestures are not merely decoration; they are integral to the prayer.
4 The liturgy is not an arbitrary collection of parts: it must be considered and experienced as a whole.

Liturgical renewal is not merely a matter of removing anomalies, for example, minor adjustments such as moving the altar from the wall, or a bit of flexibility for different pastoral situations, or the involvement of lay ministers, or even the revising of rites or the authorization of a new Prayer Book. These are all valuable, but they are surface expressions of the real issue. These external factors are a summons to serious corporate prayer. How do we make that summons live?

The authentic liturgical act is not a luxury for the Church. It is decisive, critical and formative; it is the bloodstream of the Body of Christ. It is not a question merely of effective or well-planned ritual. It is an act which reveals what the Church is. For example, there was once a style of celebration of the Eucharist in which the priest did virtually everything. This was an icon, an expression, a sign of the Church's self-understanding: the Eucharist was a cultic act under the complete authority of the officials, the ordained clergy. It was conformed to the authorized books and rules, and it was observed by an essentially passive lay congregation who were essentially involved in an act of private devotion.

The danger for us today would be to see lay involvement merely as the current liturgical fashion. For some there might be a nostalgia for the old style, for others an enthusiasm for the new; but both views are capable of remaining on the surface of the matter and seeing the question only in terms of a favoured liturgical style. What lies behind the now familiar liturgical changes, however, is an awareness of the relation of the liturgy to the Church's identity. The question of the involvement of a diversity of lay ministers, for example, is really the issue of a true mutuality and reciprocity of ministers within the Body of Christ.

It is a real *doing* only if it evidently and in experience corresponds to what is going on in the life of the congregation in the complementarity of ministries. It cannot merely be said from the pulpit, nor 'staged' in the liturgy, or else it remains at the surface of the real issue. The inner sense must be revealed in the outward signs: having connections with the life experience, not fossilized religious gestures. The authentic liturgical act is a truly communal act; full participation is not the coinciding of the private piety of isolated individuals, but an integration of all the gathered individuals into a single act, as members of one Body. The liturgical act should constantly call each one of us back to a sense of membership in the Church, membership in the Body, membership in the people of God. If sin is often a prideful turning in upon ourselves, to our needs, our concerns, our priorities, then grace calls us outward to the other person in his or her needs, concerns, or priorities. In an extraordinary way, the other person looked upon in Christ calls me out of my narrow self to my true self, the self fulfilled in the mystery of our common life.

This is not the liturgical piety which has formed most of us. An individualized piety still dominates even in many places where a more corporate liturgical experience is celebrated each Sunday, because piety is deeply sub-rational. The filter of an individualized piety interprets the experience as much as possible in terms of the former mentality. New rites often indicate an external side of a shift of piety which has not taken place at the individual, interior level. Re-education is imperative: we need to learn a new experience of the liturgy, an experience connected with daily life experience. We must read the liturgical experience in a new way, not with our faces in a book; liturgy is not merely a set of printed words. Active participation involves far more than merely following the ritual in a book or even attentive listening. Active participation extends from the liturgical act into the realities of daily life. Without that, the reforms of rites and texts, important as they are, will not really effect the necessary change. The liturgy is the fundamental common act of Christians; it is not merely sitting together in a building for an hour, even if the rites are the most beautiful or edifying that we can imagine. We are called together because of a solidarity of existence.

We humans share in common a brief life-span on earth; how do we as Christians bring the Gospel to bear upon that common life? Where do we look for the signs of social transformation for which we are called to be agents through our membership in the Body of Christ? In his foreword to a book on the social implications of the Eucharist, Roman Catholic Bishop Leo Nanayakkara, of Sri Lanka, writes, 'this most liberative act has been so domesticated by a socio-economic system that it now enslaves and domesticates its participants.'[33] This is strong language, but can we hear the truth in it? Is the bishop not saying that the Eucharist as a privatized act of devotion is robbed of its transforming power, locking us into a pattern of soothing religious rituals which protect and shield us from the social imperatives of the Eucharist in its true meaning? If we want to understand the social consequences of the Eucharist, what is required is a radical conversion, a cleansing of the inherited liturgical mentality. We must face the agonizing question of why, with our rediscovery of the centrality of the communal act of Christian identity in the Eucharist, *why* do we fail by and large to recognize the judgement it brings upon us as individual believers, as an institution in society, and as a community of witness to Jesus Christ in the world? The gaps in income, property, education, health, and power grow more serious daily, and seem virtually immune to some direct Christian confrontation except for that of a few heroic individuals and groups. How is it that a people who proclaim their unity in the bread broken and shared remain helpless and virtually uncritical of a socio-economic system which deprives the poor of bread and of all the other requirements of human life and dignity?

We are all shaped by our social and cultural circumstances. This conditioning is obvious, but its full impact is not easily recognized. It is not merely that people in the First World nations, for example, enjoy a higher standard of living than the people of the Third World, but that these privileged circumstances affect our understanding of Christian faith and worship. Our situation radically conditions our perceptions. Our habits, our cultural environment, the social structures and patterns which we take for granted, have created what we might call 'moral blinkers'. By and large, we have little sense of the moral imperatives which flow from the Sunday assembly in which we celebrate the liberation given to us in the Passover of Christ from death to life. The eucharistic celebration is a celebration of this human liberation and solidarity won for us in Christ, and we act it out in a sharing of the broken bread and the life-giving cup. Yet these ethical implications do not get through; the connection is not made. A major reason is that our individualized piety has shaped our perceptions of the Sunday eucharistic assembly, so that in it we are shielded rather than confronted.

THE SOCIAL SIGNIFICANCE OF THE EUCHARISTIC RITE

If we can consider anew the structure of the Eucharist, we find a symbolic action with considerable social significance. First, in the liturgy of the Word, in the proclamation of scripture, the continual challenge is to hear the Word, truly to hear. The goal of this part of any liturgy is not merely that the words spoken be heard. Audibility of the proclaimed Word is only a first step to hearing in a much deeper sense. The goal of the proclamation of scripture and of preaching is the experience of meaning, the opening up of a fuller perception of truth. This type of proclamation comes to us always as a judgement upon our complacency about things as they are and reminds us of what they are called by God to be, and how we are called as instruments of that purpose. This type of proclamation always offers us a choice: to live according to the fuller perception which has been opened up for us, or else to revert to the security of things as they are, the injustice, the indifference.

This points precisely to the way a highly individualized piety has shaped our experience of the liturgy. It is often said that the current standard of preaching is low. The full picture is somewhat more complex. I have often heard powerful and insightful preaching, and I have the impression that there is at least a reasonable frequency of such preaching. But our inherited attitude toward the liturgical act reflects a kind of schizoid state. We hear, but do not really *hear*. The liturgy is an encapsulated experience, entered into in isolation from real human experiences. It does not connect with the real world because it has been shaped by a piety which is often consciously an escape from the pressures of the real world. Liturgical time is seen as 'holy time' working according to its own laws, and feeding our hunger and thirst for God. But it does not connect for the great majority of our people with the real choices of daily life. Liturgical time *is* holy time. But this is a deceptive idea if we do not see what it means. Liturgical time is holy time not because it is untainted by real human experience, but because it is revelatory time. It is the time we take out from the limitations of our often rigid daily patterns and the constraints which they impose and in which God reveals the divine presence in the most ordinary realities of human life.

This is the key to the transforming power of an authentic liturgical act. It reveals to us again and again that even now, in all that is most painfully human, God is with us and that we are his instruments for the transformation of the whole fabric of human life. Prior to the moment of that hearing which is so much more than passive listening or a dislocated spiritual reflection, prior to that hearing,

97

our lives continue to be controlled by the attitudes and systems of our culture. If the liturgy does not break through those limitations, we come to identify reality with what is in fact a very small portion of the real world. The moment of a true hearing of the Word begins or renews the process of conversion, and thus throws all the complacent views shaped by our culture into question. There are many elements in the liturgy which may precipitate this experience: a gesture, a hymn, a sense of presence, but the readings and the preaching are part of the liturgical act with that specific purpose. This should indicate to us the care with which this first major part of the Eucharist should be prepared. It must not be domesticated into a merely ritual routine.

The Bible speaks to us of social oppression, the sufferings of human beings, the harm of economic injustice, the effects of prejudice and hatred; but, sad to say, these have seldom been the content of much of our preaching. Perhaps that is what is most seriously wrong with preaching. It is too narrowly 'churchy' in theme and not sufficiently biblical. As we are able to correct that, the suffering and hunger of people around the world will cease to be a painful moment on our TV screens and will become the imperative we recognize when our own sisters or brothers are oppressed or threatened with annihilation. Here we begin to sense the social implications of the liturgy. It impels us to action; it overflows into all the choices of our daily lives.

The Bible in the liturgy is a reminder that the quality of our responsibility and the pattern of our service have a decisive impact in determining the good fruit which our attempts to address the needs of human beings may bear. We do not have infallible answers. We often must take steps of service along a dark path. We must not be too authoritarian in determining what the goals should be, because we are involved in the mystery of God's ways with his people. The integrity of our steps, the quality and good which should characterize the means we use are the areas of our stewardship and responsibility.

Our new life under the reign of God finds a complementary expression in the eucharistic meal. Our common life in Christ is proclaimed by rites and gestures, movements and signs, words and touch, by honour shown equally to all, and above all in our eating and drinking the holy gifts together. Just as the word is proclaimed to all who will listen, without regard to status, so the eucharistic feast is offered to all who have been baptized into the new life, without distinctions of nationality, class, sex, colour, wealth, power, or family. If we take this sign seriously, its social implications are staggering. We have here a model for a genuinely Christian society in its acknowledgement of the reign of God over human history. This model has the wonderful flexibility of a story told and retold to which each generation adds its voice, not suffocated by the heavy hand of the past, yet living upon the nourishment offered by the tradition.

If we have eyes to see, the liturgy places us in a new situation. It opens up for us a new kind of existence in which we are, quite simply, the children of God: all sinners, all loved, and with the world's distinctions put aside. The different roles are differences of mutual service within the community, not differences of superiority or inferiority, of domination or submission. By Baptism we are all equally members of the Body. Where else in this world but in the Eucharist are king and beggar given the same gifts? Where else in this world but in the Eucharist are food and drink blessed in a common prayer of thanksgiving and given equally to all?

We died with Christ in Baptism so that we might live in him, and in each Eucharist we celebrate the mystery of life through death. Does this enable us to see the radical social consequences of the liturgy as an expression of God's perpetual work of transformation, breaking down only so that he may build anew? Such ideas require an expansion of our inherited sense of the meaning of the sacraments in liturgical worship. In these acts the members of the Church are offered a means of contact with the whole range of God's activity in the world. Through a common language of word and gesture, and utilizing the basic natural elements of human washing and nourishment, we share in acts of the most profound significance, affirming the presence of a loving God who calls us into an all-encompassing unity of love and service as his own people.

12   Conclusion

The word 'piety' has appeared many times in this book. It is a word which probably has various associations in the minds of the readers, and not all those associations are positive. It can evoke the image of a type of temperament which is preoccupied with devotion to religious activities and attitudes, and not much concerned with worldly matters. The word, however, acquired an important association with the renewal of the Church's liturgical understanding because of its use in the title of an influential book which was published almost thirty years ago.

Louis Bouyer's *Liturgical Piety* appeared in 1955, and for many people it marked a turning point in their understanding of the nature of the liturgy. Father Bouyer there distinguishes what he calls 'objective' as contrasted with 'subjective' piety. The book indicates the need for the integration of both these dimensions for the wholeness of the liturgical act, but recognizes that the fundamental liturgical error which developed from the Middle Ages is found in the gradual domination of the subjective dimensions of piety. For Bouyer, the authentic spirit of the liturgy requires a balance of the two. He traces the shift from an integrated piety which he associates with the liturgical worship of approximately the first six centuries to the emergence of a primacy of the subjective spirit from the late seventh century onwards. This shift parallels the accompanying shift of emphasis from a corporate sense of the Church's relation with God to a concern for the union of the individual with him. The individualism reflected in a highly subjective piety has continued to dominate the understanding of the Christian life until our own time, and it is only now that liturgical renewal is summoning Christians to a recovery of the balance of a truly ecclesial piety. It is remarkable how easily subjective piety found a home in widely differing theological traditions, both Catholic and Protestant.

The concern for the recovery of an objective balance to the subjective aspect is in no sense an opposition to personal devotion, but is rather the affirmation that a healthy Christian piety must first acknowledge that the central content of the liturgical act is the paschal mystery, that is, the redeeming act of God in Christ. That primary reality is renewed and shared by the Church through the liturgical celebration, which is the point at which the subjectivity of the specific local gathering of the faithful becomes experientially engaged by God's reaching out toward his creation through the instrument of the liturgical signs. Authentic liturgy depends upon this living and interior action of God as the basis of its meaning rather than upon the official regulation of external aspects of worship by the clergy. Subjective piety must not be permitted to turn in upon itself, but rather must be nurtured by the objective substance of Christian faith.

The Tractarians were concerned to reaffirm within Anglicanism the objective content of the Catholic faith which they saw as fundamental to Christianity. Their emphasis upon sacramental instrumentality was an expression of their conviction about the objective reality of God's grace which is communicated through the sacramental rites. In this area, as we have seen, their ideas ran counter to the rationalism which denied to Christianity the element of mystery which sacramentalism presumed. At the same time, their affirmation of the potential of material things to be instruments of grace implied a rejection of what they saw as the unbalanced interiority of evangelical piety.

Following Bouyer's approach, we may say that authentic Christian piety involves both the objective and subjective dimensions. This balance corresponds completely to the sacramental nature of the Church and its articulation in the entire sacramental system. The sacraments first signify

God's action toward mankind, but also require a specific community of faith, sensitive to the realities of their human situation, in which that saving action of God can take root. That community of faith, the local church in union with all the local churches throughout the world, is the primary field of God's activity. Just as the acts of salvation history were performed with reference to a people, it is through membership in that people that individual believers become heirs of the promised gifts. It is the church, not the individual believer, which is the *normative* agent for Christian liturgical worship.

We need to consider the word 'normative' as used in regard to liturgical matters. Much of what has been implied in the views presented in this book does not correspond to what many Christians have commonly experienced in worship. The most obvious example is the private or semi-private context in which countless baptisms of infants have taken place. Yet the theology of Baptism which is emerging in general ecumenical consensus suggests an ecclesial concept of its meaning: incorporation into the community of the faithful expressed through a clearly corporate liturgical celebration. Which pattern is normative, the ecclesial model or the model which Christians have experienced in small gatherings of family and friends in a corner of the parish church on a Sunday afternoon?

Aidan Kavanagh has shed valuable light on the question of what is or is not normative. He presents his concept of a norm as requiring:

> that the Church be palpably manifested in all its splendid variety and ministerial diversity in all its sacramental deeds — but especially in eucharistic celebrations, which are the mode in which the Church itself most regularly assembles. The norm means not that the bishop must preside at every Mass, even if this were possible. It does mean, however, that in both theory and practice the eucharist is never to be regarded as anything less than an act of the whole Church, head and members, and that this *norm* must

103

to some extent always be achieved, even when the chief pastor of the local church does not himself preside. The eucharist is never a matter of a bishop's or a presbyter's own feelings or piety alone: it is never 'his Mass'. Nor is the sacrifice of the New Covenant ever merely a matter of contractual obligation between private parties in the Church. Rather, it is always the Church being most itself in public, obedient to the Lord's command to 'do this for my remembrance', in a manner worthy of his Body at once ecclesial and sacramental.

Applying this approach to our question as to whether baptisms celebrated apart from a gathering of the local church can be considered normative, the answer must be an unqualified 'No'. Baptism is not an event which concerns only the parents and the immediate family; it is an act of the Church, and its celebration must *normatively* manifest that meaning. As Father Kavanagh goes on to say, underlying this concept of norm 'is a wholly crucial theology of faith that is actualized constantly in communal events both sacramental in nature and ecclesial in scope. No event that may occur apart from this norm, no matter how usual or frequent, can be anything but abnormal to some degree.'

For generations, liturgical practice has failed to meet this standard, and consequently the understanding of the meaning of the sacramental rites has been mis-shaped through the influence of these repeated patterns. Liturgical and sacramental integrity compels us to reawaken among both laity and clergy an awareness of the underlying normative meaning. Kavanagh continues,

A *norm* in this sense has nothing to do with the number of times a thing is done, but it has everything to do with the standard according to which a thing is done. So long as the norm is in place both in practice and in the awareness of those who are engaged in it, the situation is capable of being judged 'normal' even though the norm must be departed from to some extent, even frequently, due to exigencies of time, place, pastoral considerations, physical inabilities, or whatever. Yet to the extent possible, the norm must always be achieved to some extent lest it slip imperceptibly into the status of a mere 'ideal' all wish for but are under no obligation to realize.[34]

Much of contemporary renewal is based upon the conviction that the authentic norms of sacramental worship had become so dangerously obscured that serious misunderstandings of sacramental meaning were permitted to develop, and, most seriously of all, that there had been a loss of a sense that it is the whole Church which acts in Christian worship. Liturgical renewal is a summons to the Church as a whole to re-establish a clear sense and practice of the normative models. In all this, the contribution of the Tractarians working within a liturgically impoverished situation was in many ways prophetic of the concerns which stand before us now. Above all, their emphasis upon the theology of the Church and its sacramental nature serves as a foundation for the views of Bouyer and Kavanagh and the whole range of contemporary liturgical writers. The Church is the primary sacrament of God's work in Christ, and is thus the instrument of grace for human redemption. The implications of that are far-reaching in significance. Liturgical acts are not, in such a perspective, to be isolated as a distinct category of religious activity but are signs of human participation in the redemptive process throughout the whole creation. For this, our worship is not a matter merely of mental or moral attitudes but of the involvement of all that is human in a response to God's gracious gift.

Notes

1 *The Ecclesiologist*, IV, pp. 49—50.
2 Ibid., V, p. 52.
3 Ibid., III, p. 134.
4 James White, *The Cambridge Movement*, pp. 52—3.
5 'Church Architecture', in *Christian Remembrancer*, III (1842), pp. 356—7.
6 *The Gothic Revival*, p. 237.
7 *Hierologus*, (London, 1843), p. 71.
8 Tracts for the Times, no. 74, offers an extraordinary series of citations in support of the theory of Apostolic Succession.
9 Sermon I of twelve sermons on 'The True Nature of the Christian Church, the Office of its Ministers, etc.', in *Works*, Library of Anglo-Catholic Theology, vol. 1, pp. 10—11.
10 *Treatise on the Church of Christ*, vol. 1, 3rd edn.; London, 1842, pp. 140—2.
11 Sermon XVII, in *Parochial Sermons*, vol. 3, p. 266.
12 Ibid., p. 268.
13 Sermon XVI, in *Parochial Sermons*, vol. 3, p. 248.
14 MS Sermon 213: 'On the Duty of Public Worship', in the Oratory, Edgbaston; quoted by A. Härdelin, *The Tractarian Understanding of the Eucharist*, p. 75.
15 MS Sermon 176: 'On the Christian Scheme of Mediation as Connected with the Natural and Jewish Systems', in the Oratory, Edgbaston; cf. discussion in A. Härdelin, *The Tractarian Understanding of the Eucharist*, pp. 67 ff.
16 R.I. Wilberforce: *The Doctrine of the Incarnation of our Lord Jesus Christ, in its Relation to Mankind and to the Church.* London (1892 edn.), pp. 212—3.
17 E.g. Tract 78, p. 7.
18 Tracts for the Times, vol. 2, 'Advertisment', pp. v—vi.
19 Tract 67 (2nd edn., 1839), pp. 81, 83.
20 Sermon XIX, in *Parochial Sermons*, vol. 3, p. 302.
21 Ibid., pp. 305—6.

22 1838 edn., pp. 259–60. Cf. Tract 90, no. 2.

23 Richard Hooker, *The Laws of Ecclesiastical Polity*, Book V, ch. 67, no. 12.

24 *The High Church Tradition* by G.W.O. Addleshaw offers a useful survey of their views.

25 The finest study of the eucharistic doctrine of the Tractarians is found in Alf Härdelin's *The Tractarian Understanding of the Eucharist*; cf. his discussion of R.I. Wilberforce's teaching, pp. 141–7, 162–8. Cf. *The Eucharistic Doctrine of the Oxford Movement*, by W.H. Mackean (London, 1933), who writes from an Evangelical and rather unsympathetic perspective.

26 *Doctrine of the Holy Eucharist* (1853), pp. 15–16.

27 *Hierologus* (London, 1843), p. 71.

28 Cf. J. Wickham Legg, *English Church Life from the Restoration to the Tractarian Movement*, pp. 351–81.

29 *A Few Words of Hope on the Present Crisis of the English Church* (London, 1850), p. 6.

30 *Baptism, Eucharist and Ministry*, Faith and Order Paper no. 111 (Geneva: World Council of Churches, 1982) ('Ministry' I/5).

31 'Our Present Duty', in *Report of the Anglo-Catholic Congress* (London, 1923), pp. 185–6. Bishop Weston's speech was presented at this second Anglo-Catholic Congress which was consciously connected with the ninetieth anniversary of the Oxford Movement.

32 *Parochial Sermons*, (Oxford, 1852), vol. 1, pp. 58–9.

33 *The Eucharist and Human Liberation*, by Tissa Balasuriya (Maryknoll: Orbis Books, 1979), p. ix.

34 *The Shape of Baptism*, pp. 107–8.

Further Reading

Addleshaw, G. W. O., *The High Church Tradition*, Faber & Faber, London, 1941

Brilioth, Yngve, *The Anglican Revival: Studies in the Oxford Movement*, Longmans Green, London, 1933

Brown, Raymond E., *Priest and Bishop*, Paulist Press, New York, 1970

Chadwick, Owen, *The Mind of the Oxford Movement*, A. & C. Black, London, 1960

Chadwick, Owen, *The Victorian Church*, A. & C. Black, London, 1971, vol. 1, esp. pp. 212–21

Church, R. W., *The Oxford Movement: Twelve Years 1833–1845*, Macmillan, London, 1982

Clark, Kenneth, *The Gothic Revival*, Holt, Rinehart and Winston, New York, 1962

Fairweather, Eugene R. (ed.), *The Oxford Movement*, Oxford University Press, New York, 1964

Guzie, Tad W., *Jesus and the Eucharist*, Paulist Press, New York, 1974

Härdelin, Alf, *The Tractarian Understanding of the Eucharist*, Almqvist and Wiksells, Uppsala, Sweden, 1965

Hellwig, Monika K., *The Eucharist and the Hunger of the World*, Paulist Press, New York, 1976

Holmes, Urban T., III, *Confirmation: the Celebration of Maturity in Christ*, Seabury Press, New York, 1975

Kavanagh, Aidan, *The Shape of Baptism: the Rite of Christian Initiation*, Pueblo Publishing, New York, 1978

Kavanagh, Aidan and others, *Made, Not Born*, University of Notre Dame Press, Notre Dame, 1976

Legg, J. Wickham, *English Church Life from the Restoration to the Tractarian Movement*, Longmans Green, London, 1914

Schillebeeckx, Edward, *Ministry: Leadership in the Community of Jesus Christ*, Crossroad, New York, 1981

Searle, Mark and others, *Liturgy and Social Justice*, Liturgical Press, Collegeville, 1980

Seasoltz, R. Kevin (ed.), *Living Bread, Saving Cup*, Liturgical Press, Collegeville, 1982

Taylor, Michael J. (ed.), *The Sacraments*, Alba House, New York, 1981

Toon, Peter, *Evangelical Theology 1833—1856: A Response to Tractarianism*, Marshall, Morgan and Scott, London, 1979

Vaillancourt, Raymond, *Toward a Renewal of Sacramental Theology*, Liturgical Press, Collegeville, 1979

White, James F., *The Cambridge Movement*, Cambridge University Press, Cambridge, 1979

Index

114